ROB DE JONGH

Psalms

Food for thought in the Old Testament series

First published by Woodland Press Ltd 2020

Copyright © 2020 by Rob de Jongh

All rights reserved. No part of this publication may be reproduced, stored or transmitted in any form or by any means, electronic, mechanical, photocopying, recording, scanning, or otherwise without written permission from the publisher. It is illegal to copy this book, post it to a website, or distribute it by any other means without permission.

Scripture quotations from the Authorized (King James) Version. Rights in the Authorized Version in the United Kingdom are vested in the Crown. Reproduced by permission of the Crown's patentee, Cambridge University Press.

Contributions by Peter L. Forbes used by kind permission.

First edition

ISBN: 978-1-913699-02-4

This book was professionally typeset on Reedsy. Find out more at reedsy.com

Contents

Introduction	xvi
Reading with your family	xvii
Leading discussion groups	xvii
Preparing a Bible talk or lecture	xvii
Preparing a sermon or exhortation	xviii
Aiding personal Bible study	xviii
How not to use this book!	xviii
Food for thought in Psalms	xx

I Psalms 1-41

Psalm 1	3
Works vs Growth	3
Psalm 2	5
Kiss the son, lest he be angry	5
Psalm 3	8
Sleeping peacefully	8
Psalm 4	11
Thou hast enlarged my steps	11
Psalm 5	14
Get the inside right first	14
Psalm 6	16
Let my enemies be ashamed	16
Psalm 7	18
What if I were judged according to my righteousness?	18
Psalm 8	20

Out of the mouth of babes and sucklings	20
Psalm 9	23
God makes inquisition for bloodshed	23
Psalm 10	25
Does God allow the poor to be oppressed?	25
Psalm 11	27
The LORD will deliver the righteous	27
Psalm 12	29
Hiding hatred with lying lips	29
Psalm 13	31
Singing to the LORD in times of trouble	31
Psalm 14	33
A repeated Psalm	33
Psalm 15	35
What kind of person will dwell with God?	35
Psalm 16	37
When is no inheritance a better inheritance?	37
Psalm 17	40
A prayer when life seems hard	40
Psalm 18	43
How the Bible works: Dual applications	43
Psalm 19	46
Presumptuous sins	46
Psalm 20	49
Chariots of mire	49
Psalm 21	51
Saying thank-you for answered prayers	51
Psalm 22	53
All they that see	53
Psalm 23	55
What was David scared of in the Valley of Death?	55

Psalm 24	57
Righteousness by faith or by effort?	57
Psalm 25	59
Learning God's way during trials	59
Psalm 26	61
How could David love God's house before it was ever built?	61
I've done it!	62
Psalm 27	64
Dwelling in God's house	64
Psalm 28	67
God will be a shield to those who trust in Him	67
Psalm 29	69
The voice of the LORD upon the waters	69
Psalm 30	72
David and Job: brothers in affliction	72
Psalm 31	74
Prophecy of Jesus or for Jesus?	74
Psalm 32	77
The joy of forgiveness	77
David's thoughts on Noah's deliverance	78
Psalm 33	80
God knows the hearts of kings and princes	80
Psalm 34	82
Taste and see that the LORD is good	82
Answered prayer builds faith	83
Psalm 35	85
Joab's net	85
Psalm 36	88
How God rewards the humble with wisdom	88
Psalm 37	94

What it means to be a child of God	94
Psalm 38	96
Can illness come because of sin?	96
Psalm 39	100
"I am consumed by the blow of thine hand"	100
Psalm 40	102
How the Psalms explain the Parables and sayings of Jesus	102
Psalm 41	105
The friend who lifted his heel against David	105

II Psalms 42-72

Psalm 42	111
Why have You forgotten me?	111
Psalm 43	114
Thy Holy Hill	114
Psalm 44	116
Standing aside from rebellion	116
Psalm 45	119
Like father like son	119
Psalm 46	121
Taking refuge in God	121
Psalm 47	123
Sing praises with understanding	123
Psalm 48	125
How the Psalms interpret Old Testament events	125
Psalm 49	128
Understanding	128
Can we pay our own ransom?	129
Psalm 50	131

Judge not, that ye be not judged	131
Psalm 51	133
What comes after forgiveness?	133
Psalm 52	135
The price of fighting against God	135
Psalm 53	137
The days of Noah repeated	137
Psalm 54	139
Betrayed by strangers	139
Psalm 55	141
Condemn not, that ye be not condemned	141
Psalm 56	144
The Giants of Gath	144
What happened to David in Gath?	145
Psalm 57	147
Resisting fierce opposition	147
Psalm 58	150
The deaf snake	150
Psalm 59	152
They lie in wait for my soul	152
Psalm 60	155
O God, thou hast cast us off	155
Psalm 61	158
How to become a child of God	158
Psalm 62	161
David's parable of the rock	161
Psalm 63	163
Worshippers of things	163
A dry and thirsty land	165
Psalm 64	167
Words that pierce like arrows	167

Psalm 65	169
A prophecy of the chosen one	169
Psalm 66	171
I will pay my vows	171
Psalm 67	174
Who else served Israel's God?	174
Psalm 68	176
God's glory shown in might and gentleness	176
What did Israel drink in the wilderness journey?	177
Psalm 69	179
A pattern for prayer in distress	179
Psalm 70	182
Learn of me, for I am meek	182
Psalm 71	185
Showing God to the next generation	185
Psalm 72	187
Prophecies of Solomon's reign	187

III Psalms 73-89

Psalm 73	191
Drawing near to God	191
Psalm 74	194
When God is against us	194
Psalm 75	197
The cup of dregs	197
Psalm 76	199
Instilling fear in the nations	199
Psalm 77	201
The chief musician	201
Psalm 78	204
If God has helped you before, why wouldn't He help again?	204
Do we limit God?	205
Psalm 79	207
The destruction of Jerusalem	207
Psalm 80	209
The vineyard	209
Psalm 81	212
Listen!	212
Psalm 82	214
Defend the poor and fatherless	214
Psalm 83	216
Ten nations	216
Psalm 84	218
Coming through the valley of weeping	218
Psalm 85	220
Turn away from folly	220
Psalm 86	222

God is ready to forgive	222
Psalm 87	224
Dwelling in Zion	224
Psalm 88	227
Jonah's Psalm	227
Psalm 89	229
Who can calm the waves of the sea?	229

IV Psalms 90-106

Psalm 90	233
Threescore years and ten	233
Psalm 91	236
Under His wings shalt thou trust	236
Psalm 92	238
Dwelling in the house of the LORD	238
Psalm 93	242
Explaining the symbol of the sea and the waves	242
Psalm 94	245
God, to whom vengeance belongs	245
Psalm 95	247
Will we ever see God?	247
Psalm 96	250
Sing a new song	250
Psalm 97	252
Ye that love the LORD, hate evil	252
Psalm 98	254
Jerusalem exalted above the hills	254
Psalm 99	257
Intercessors	257
Psalm 100	259

When all the earth will make a joyful noise	259
Psalm 101	262
David removes the deceitful from his presence	262
Psalm 102	265
Heavens and the earth: A key to prophetic Scripture	265
Psalm 103	268
The son's repentance and father's forgiveness	268
David's Illness	269
Psalm 104	270
He laid the foundations of the earth	270
Psalm 105	272
What is the result of faith in the promises?	272
Psalm 106	274
A prayer echoed through Israel's history	274

V Psalm 107-150

Psalm 107	279
Oh that men would praise the LORD for His goodness!	279
Psalm 108	281
Why did David go to fight Edom?	281
Psalm 109	283
In response to my love, they are my adversaries	283
Psalm 110	285
The beheaded heifer	285
Psalm 111	289
Wisdom starts somewhere, but it doesn't finish there	289
Psalm 112	291
Giving to the poor and allowing God to reimburse	291
Psalm 113	294
Hannah's prayer	294
Psalm 114	296
God's presence during the Exodus from Egypt	296
Psalm 115	298
Three Psalms that overlap	298
Psalm 116	300
How God trained David	300
Psalm 117	302
If only they had read this properly	302
Psalm 118	304
They compassed me about	304
Psalm 119:1-40	306
How to deal with sinful thoughts	306
Psalm 119:41-80	308
The wonderful liberty given by God's precepts	308
Psalm 119:81-120	310

Words that live forever	310
Psalm 119:129-176	312
Lost and alone inside our consciousness	312
Psalm 120	314
I am for peace… they are for war	314
Psalm 121	316
When the sun moved backwards	316
Psalm 122	318
Let us go into the house of the LORD	318
Psalm 123	320
The scorn of those that are at ease	320
Psalm 124	322
Passing over the Jordan	322
Psalm 125	324
Mount Zion cannot be moved	324
Psalm 126	326
The captivity of Zion	326
Psalm 127	328
Men whose teeth are spears and arrows	328
Psalm 128	330
Does God really bless those who walk in His ways?	330
Psalm 129	332
The youth of the nation of Israel	332
Psalm 130	334
God does not keep hold of our sins	334
Psalm 131	336
Lifted up in pride	336
Psalm 132	338
David's vow: to house the Ark of the Covenant	338
Psalm 133	340
The blessing of life for evermore	340

Psalm 134	342
In the house of the LORD by night	342
Psalm 135	345
For I know that the LORD is great	345
Psalm 136	347
O give thanks to the LORD, for His mercy endureth forever	347
Psalm 137	349
Edom's hatred of Jerusalem	349
Psalm 138	351
A matter of perspective	351
Psalm 139	353
Thine eyes did see my substance	353
Psalm 140	356
How to act towards people who hate you	356
Psalm 141	358
Trusting in God when depressed	358
Psalm 142	360
Deliver me from my persecutors, for they are stronger than I	360
Psalm 143	362
Being justified (made righteous)	362
Psalm 144	365
The LORD my Rock	365
Psalm 145	368
Proclaim God's goodness	368
Psalm 146	371
Which God do you mean?	371
Psalm 147	374
A message for the invisible people	374
Psalm 148	377

Praising God	377
Psalm 149	380
The two-edged sword	380
Psalm 150	383
Praise God in His sanctuary	383
Epilogue	387
Other books in the series	388
Index	390
About the Author	410

Introduction

When Jesus taught us to pray "give us today our daily bread", he wasn't talking about food, but the word of God. He said:

Man shall not live by bread alone, but by every word of God.

When Jesus met Peter after his resurrection and told Peter to feed the believers, he didn't mean with fish, but with the word of God:

So when they had dined, Jesus saith to Simon Peter, Simon, son of Jonas, lovest thou me more than these? He saith unto him, Yea, Lord; thou knowest that I love thee. He saith unto him, Feed my lambs.

Finding time to read the word of God can be difficult, and teaching it to others can seem an impossible task. Many of us simply *find ourselves* teaching the Bible, either at home to our life partner, or to our children, or as lay teachers or ministers or group leaders, without any training or resources.

Using the *Food for Thought in the Old Testament* series gives you a framework of Bible thoughts for each chapter of the Bible, allowing you to start discussion, create Bible talks and sermons, or simply to meditate on or dig deeper in your own study.

Reading with your family

If you are reading a chapter of the Bible at home with your family, first choose a chapter and read it together, preferably reading out loud (perhaps in sections of 2, 5 or 10 verses each) so that everyone gets a chance to join in. You can then find the relevant chapter in *Food for Thought in Psalms* and read one or more of the thoughts for that chapter. When you encounter a Bible reference, ask someone to turn it up and read it. Once you have finished, there may be questions in the text to answer, or the passage may have provided *food for thought* for further discussion.

Leading discussion groups

If you are leading a Bible discussion group, you could start by reading a chapter of the Bible around the group, followed by your presenting a short introduction of the chapter based on the relevant section of *Food for Thought in Psalms*. Once that is done, open up the group for discussion about any topics raised by the Bible chapter or in your introductory thoughts.

Preparing a Bible talk or lecture

If you are preparing a Bible talk or lecture, *Food for Thought in Psalms* can be used to piece your talk together using several sections of the book, or several books in the series. For example, for a Bible study on "refuge", use the eBook search feature or paperback index to list any sections including references to "refuge". Piece together any sections that you think go well together, then read those sections and follow the Bible references in your Bible. Finally, put your discoveries down in your own words and practice at least once before presenting them.

Preparing a sermon or exhortation

For a talk/sermon or more motivational style thought, start with a topic from the contents list at the start of the book. Focus on the personal questions thrown up by that section, and spend time exploring what the Bible characters in that section were feeling, based on what we are told in the Bible chapter and any references provided in this book. Read out plenty of Scripture during your talk to illuminate what that character was like and what they went through.

Aiding personal Bible study

For your own personal Bible study, it is often helpful to start somewhere (anywhere is better than nowhere!) and follow where the path leads. *Food for Thought in Psalms* can help with this by providing many links to related Bible passages. Any of these will be well worth looking at to see how they relate to the partner passage in Psalms. Once you have two or more related passages, read over the context of each in your Bible and see what questions and conclusions jump out. Now follow other referenced passages out of those chapters, and so on.

How not to use this book!

This book series is not an explanation of the whole Old Testament. To do that would take a million pages. Many people have foolishly tried to create books like that, and failed. Reference works on the Bible are seldomly productive for Bible students, since they can stifle your ability to read the Word and make your own conclusions based on what you read.

Remember what we started the introduction with? The Bible is for food, not just for knowledge. Jesus asked Peter to feed, not people, but lambs and sheep. In other words, the Bible text is to be eaten, chewed over, and meditated on, in a similar way to how sheep chew over their food.

Rumination is the key to understanding the Old Testament.

This book is a collection of starting points, one or more for each chapter of the Psalms. May God bless you as you step off from these onto your own journey through the scriptures.

Food for thought in Psalms

Who knows what you or I are thinking when we go through our most challenging times? Only ourselves and God. But what if we were able to look into someone else's mind? What would we see? And would we see a mirror of our own thoughts and feelings there?

David went through some of the most extreme events we can think of. Persecution, murder attempts on his life, fighting a giant, marrying a princess, becoming a king… and in all of this, his thoughts are written down for us to read.

The Psalms are a wonderful accompaniment to the Old Testament events recorded in the books of 1 & 2 Samuel, 1 & 2 Kings, and 1 & 2 Chronicles. They show what David, Solomon and Hezekiah were thinking at the most challenging times of their lives. They show us the prayers they were offering, and the answers they received. They show their struggles with accepting the will of God when their human nature wanted them to rebel.

In *Food for thought in Psalms*, we look at each Psalm individually and draw out where in the rest of the Bible these words are related to. We discover how the Psalms reveal what David was thinking when Saul and his armies were surrounding him. We look at his agony over his adultery with Bathsheba. We go with him as he flees his own son and has to face betrayal by his closest friend. And we look at how these innermost thoughts relate to our own thoughts too.

But the beauty of the Psalms does not stop there, for many of the Psalms contain prophecies of the Lord Jesus Christ — the mission he was to undertake — and the agonies he was to go through in order to become the saviour of mankind.

To look into the mind of Jesus as he hung on the cross is perhaps the biggest privilege any of us can ever have, and it is by reading and understanding the Psalms that we may do so.

I

Psalms 1-41

Psalm 1

Works vs Growth

In Psalm 1, we have described for us in a nutshell, all we have to do to receive blessings from God:

> *Blessed is the man that walketh not in the counsel of the ungodly, nor standeth in the way of sinners, nor sitteth in the seat of the scornful. But his delight is in the law of the LORD; and in his law doth he meditate day and night. (Psa 1:1-2)*

Blessed is the man who:

- Doesn't walk according to the advice of the ungodly
- Doesn't hang around with sinners
- Doesn't go along with the scornful

but instead:

- Delights in the law of God
- Thinks about it all the time
- Plants himself where he can receive spiritual nourishment

I think we can all from time to time become obsessed with trying to better ourselves, and naturally we would go about that by trying to make ourselves do good works. When we do this we can become very disappointed when we fail. We sometimes measure ourselves against the example of others, or of Christ, which can make us feel unworthy or worthless.

But this is the opposite to the advice of this Psalm. The Psalm suggests that if only we remove ourselves from bad influences, and plant ourselves in good influences, then we will bear fruit of righteousness. Fruit grows automatically on that tree, as it will with us. Once we make this shift in emphasis away from work to think instead about growth, we will never feel wretched at our lack of works, because instead we will wait patiently for God to bring forth fruit in us:

> *And he shall be like a tree planted by the rivers of water, that bringeth forth his fruit in his season; his leaf also shall not wither; and whatsoever he doeth shall prosper. (Psa 1:3)*

Food for thought

Verse 1 - "Blessed is the man" is a recurring phrase in the Psalms (see Psalms 32:1, 65:4, 84:5,12, 94:12, 112:1). A review of these passages will enable us to build up a picture of how we should behave. The idea then passes into New Testament use in the Sermon on the Mount "Blessed are they ..." (Matthew 5:4,6,10).

Verse 3 - The man who is blessed whose "leaf also shall not wither" is like the everlasting trees by the water in Ezekiel's temple (Ezekiel 47:12).

Psalm 2

Kiss the son, lest he be angry

Putting Psalm 2 in its context is difficult because we don't know who wrote it, or when. While David is the author who wrote most Psalms (he was called "the sweet Psalmist of Israel" in 2 Samuel 23:1), many other authors are included too. We have some clues though. Let's take a look:

> *Why do the heathen rage, and the people imagine a vain thing? The kings of the earth set themselves, and the rulers take counsel together, against the LORD, and against his anointed, saying, Let us break their bands asunder, and cast away their cords from us. (Psalm 2:1-3)*

So it is a time where the anointed King of Israel reigns over other nations as well as Israel. Their service is not willingly offered. "let us break their bands asunder" sounds like tribute is being paid to this king.

> *Yet have I set my king upon my holy hill of Zion. (Psalm 2:6)*

This tells us the King was ruling from Jerusalem, rather than Hebron, Samaria or Gibeah as at other times.

> *Kiss the Son, lest he be angry, and ye perish from the way, when his wrath is kindled but a little. Blessed are all they that put their trust in him. (Psalm 2:12)*

This verse sounds like a father had set up the Kingdom and was passing it on to his son.

I would suggest that this Psalm may be based around the time at the end of David's reign and the beginning of Solomon's. David's military campaigns had successfully secured the borders and brought the surrounding nations into tribute. These Kings had to decide whether to continue serving and passing tribute money to Solomon, or risk war if they refused.

Some of the details in the Psalm still do not fit completely, which is why this Psalm must ultimately be a prophecy of Jesus. Jesus will reign over all the world, not just a part of it:

> *Ask of me, and I shall give thee the heathen for thine inheritance, and **the uttermost parts of the earth** for thy possession. (Psalm 2:8)*

Of him the LORD would say:

> *...Thou art my Son; this day have I begotten thee. (Psalm 2:7)*

Which is applied to Jesus in the new testament book of Hebrews:

> *For unto which of the angels said he at any time, **Thou art my Son, this day have I begotten thee**? And again, I will be to*

him a Father, and he shall be to me a Son? (Hebrews 1:5)

Food for thought

Verse 2 - We see a fulfilment of this in Matthew 27:1 when the Jewish leaders sought to crucify Jesus. Whilst at that time it appeared – for a short time – that they had achieved their ends, God will have the final word as the Psalm goes on to show.

Verse 8 - In saying "ask of me …" God is telling Jesus, in advance, that he is the heir of the world – a great antidote to the temptations he would undergo (Luke 4:6).

Psalm 3

Sleeping peacefully

In Psalm 3 and 4 David is obviously in great distress. Many times he repeats his cry for help, "save me" or "hear my cry!"

How interesting, then, that in verse 5 David says "I lay down and slept". How could someone sleep whilst in a state of such trouble and anxiety?

> *I laid me down and slept; I awaked; for the LORD sustained me. (Psa 3:5)*

Again, in Psalm 4 verse 4 he is quiet on his bed, and in v8 he says "I will both lie down in peace, and sleep"!

> *Stand in awe, and sin not: commune with your own heart upon your bed, and be still. Selah. ... I will both lay me down in peace, and sleep: for thou, LORD, only makest me dwell in safety. (Psa 4:4, 8)*

Jesus did the same thing when he was in the boat on Galilee. He was in the same trouble as the disciples, being in the same boat, yet while they were anxious, he was calmly asleep:

> *And, behold, there arose a great tempest in the sea, insomuch that the ship was covered with the waves: but he was asleep. And his disciples came to him, and awoke him, saying, Lord, save us: we perish. And he saith unto them, Why are ye fearful, O ye of little faith? Then he arose, and rebuked the winds and the sea; and there was a great calm. (Mat 8:24-26)*

So also with David. In his anxiety he called out to God. He meditated upon his knowledge of God, and realised that having asked his Father for help, he ought to believe in that help, because God had always helped him in times past. At the same time he wrote the words of these Psalms, he was probably still experiencing his problems, yet he had conquered his anxiety through faith. Therefore in Psalm 3:6 he says "I will not be afraid", and in 4:5 he advises us: "put your trust in the LORD:

> *I will not be afraid of ten thousands of people, that have set themselves against me round about. (Psa 3:6)*

> *Offer the sacrifices of righteousness, and put your trust in the LORD. (Psa 4:5)*

Having realised these things, he could confidently say "I will both lie down in peace, and sleep; For you alone, O LORD, make me dwell in safety".

Food for thought

Verse 1 (Title) The title of this Psalm tells us what historical event is remembered in the Psalm. So when David says in v8 "salvation belongeth unto the Lord" we realise that he is saying this against the background of his fear of the counsel of Ahithophel and Absalom's following.

Verse 6 - The boast that the Psalmist will not be afraid of 10,000 picks up the promise to the faithful in Israel (Leviticus 26:8).

Psalm 4

Thou hast enlarged my steps

Verse 1 appears to be a reference to Psalm 18, written about David's desperate situation at the time of his fight with the Amalekites. His wives and children, and the families of all his soldiers had been taken captive.

The specific phrase that links these two Psalms is "Thou hast enlarged me". It appears in 4:1 and 18:36 and, as we shall see, refers to the way God helped David overcome the Amalekites:

> *Hear me when I call, O God of my righteousness:* **thou hast enlarged me** *when I was in distress; have mercy upon me, and hear my prayer. (Psalm 4:1)*

In Psalm 18, that same phrase is used, and we can see exactly what this "enlarging" was:

> *"Thou hast enlarged my steps under me, that my feet did not slip. I have pursued mine enemies, and overtaken them: neither did I turn again till they were consumed. I have wounded them that they were not able to rise: they are fallen under my feet.*

For thou hast girded me with strength unto the battle: thou hast subdued under me those that rose up against me." (Psalm 18:36-39)

If we read the account of the battle in 1 Samuel 30, we see that David had literally no strength left to chase after his enemies, having only just returned from another battle front. So much was the fatigue in evidence that many of his men were physically unable to continue. Thus David requested of God:

"shall I pursue after this troop? Shall I overtake them?"

It's not that he was asking permission, but that he was asking for God's help to do so. He knew he had no strength to do this, but the need for action to save his family remained. What would you do if it were you?

We know from other passages of Scripture that God on occasion gave supernatural speed or strength to His servants, and adding these two Psalms and the account in Samuel together, we can clearly see that this was the case here. This explains David's specific wording: shall I pursue? In other words, will you give me strength to get back on the road? Shall I overtake them? In other words, will You give me speed or slow them down?

Question 1: Can you find other occasions where God helped David with strength, speed or skill?

Question 2: Do you think God would help you like this if you really needed it? What Scripture would you use to back up your opinion?

Food for thought

Verse 2 - "Selah" means "weight", in the sense of value. It is used in Job 28:16 where it is translated "valued". We should read the word when reading the Psalms, rather than skipping over it, and understand that it is an instruction in the text to value the things we have just read.

Verse 4 - "Stand in awe and sin not" – quoted in Ephesians 4:26, teaches us that an awareness of the majesty of God should help us to resist temptation, knowing that our sins damage our relationship with our Father.

Psalm 5

Get the inside right first

> *For there is no faithfulness in their mouth; their inward part is very wickedness; their throat is an open sepulchre; they flatter with their tongue. (Psa 5:9)*

Notice in verse 9 there are people who can flatter you and seem great on the outside, but "their inward part is very wickedness". Contrast this with what God requires:

> *Behold, thou desirest truth in the inward parts: and in the hidden part thou shalt make me to know wisdom. (Psa 51:6)*

This second quote was from a Psalm David wrote some time after his sin with Bathsheba, so David is not claiming to be a perfect example of virtue. What he is saying is that God wants us to be right from within, and no amount of flattery on the outside will cover a rotten inside. So also with us, we need to work on our own inner thoughts and desires first, so that the outward words and actions flow naturally from within.

Food for thought

Verse 3 - In saying that God will hear his prayer in the morning, we are given a clue that David started each day with prayer to his God.

Verse 5 - The phrase that the "foolish shall not stand" is like the "ungodly" who will not stand in Psalm 1:5. So the ungodly and fools are equated with each other. Maybe this should cause us to take care as to who we call a fool?

Psalm 6

Let my enemies be ashamed

David had always been the example of virtue and Godliness, but David had now sinned by committing adultery with another man's wife. This sin had become known openly in the palace. Over the years this had led to growing disenchantment within his own close group of advisers and friends, as some of them now despised the one they had looked up to so much. It is probably at the time just before Absalom's uprising, when trouble was simmering, that David penned these words:

> *O Lord, rebuke me not in thine anger, neither chasten me in thy hot displeasure... Let all mine enemies be ashamed and sore vexed: let them return and be ashamed suddenly. (Psa 6:1,10)*

David appears to have known that the danger to his life was acute:

> *For in death there is no remembrance of thee: in the grave who shall give thee thanks? (Psa 6:5)*

The title of the Psalm mentions Sheminith, a musical instrument, and the only other Psalm that does likewise is Psalm 12. By linking the two Psalms in this way, God means us to read them together and draw conclusions. What details can you find in Psalm 12 that give us a fuller view of what went on at this time?

Food for thought

Verse 6 - David here talks about his feelings of remorse after some terrible sin – possibly his sin with Bathsheba – and his repentance.

Verse 8 - Jesus quotes "Depart ... iniquity" in Matthew 7:23 and Luke 13:27. On both occasions he is speaking to his disciples warning them how he will deal with those who reject him at his return.

Psalm 7

What if I were judged according to my righteousness?

Which of us could pray the words of Psalm 7 to God with an honest heart?

> *If there is iniquity in my hands... Let the enemy pursue me and... trample my life to the earth. (Psa 7:3-5)*

Or:

> *... judge me, O LORD, according to my righteousness, and according to mine integrity that is in me. (Psa 7:8)*

Would we be able to utter such a prayer? Wouldn't we remember the things we had done which weren't right in His sight? Wouldn't we be afraid to be judged *according* to our righteousness, because of our lack of it? Maybe this prayer could only be made by Jesus himself. As for the rest of us, Psalm 6 might be a more advisable prayer to emulate:

Have mercy on me, O LORD, for I am weak.... Save me for your mercies sake." (Psalm 6:2-4)

God remembers that He made us from dust in the first place. He knows that if He were to judge us by our righteousness we would fail miserably. God will always accept us if in the humility of our hearts we cry to Him, having realised that our own righteousness is as dirty rags:

The LORD has heard the voice of my weeping. The LORD has heard my supplication; The LORD will receive my prayer (v.8-9)

Food for thought

Verse 6 - "Arise O Lord" is what was said when the ark moved – Num 10:35 – As we have noticed there are other quotations from the time of the wilderness journey. We may conclude that this Psalm looks to God for His deliverance as He delivered Israel in the wilderness.

Verse 3-4 - In his repeated "if" statements David is a little like Job – Job 31:5-11.

Psalm 8

Out of the mouth of babes and sucklings

> *Out of the mouth of babes and sucklings hast thou ordained strength because of thine enemies, that thou mightest still the enemy and the avenger. (Psa 8:2)*

Who are the babes mentioned in verse 2, and how did they give David strength? The heading of the Psalm says "upon Gittith", and a Gittite is someone from Gath, a Philistine city. Is it possible that this is written about the 600 Gittites that followed David and swore loyalty to him?

Clearly this is a time of great anxiety for David. The verse talks about his enemies and "the avenger". One period of time comes to mind when David was indeed in trouble, and it was at this crucial point that the Gittites came to his aid:

> *And all his servants passed on beside him; and all the Cherethites, and all the Pelethites, and all the Gittites, six hundred men which came after him from Gath, passed on before the king. (2Sa 15:18)*

The passage above is written at the time when David is fleeing his palace in Jerusalem, as his son Absalom comes to try to take the throne. As he flees David turns to the Gittites and asks them why they should come to exile with him, when they could just stay behind and be safe? Their leader answers in the most wonderful way:

And Ittai answered the king, and said, As the LORD liveth, and as my lord the king liveth, surely in what place my lord the king shall be, whether in death or life, even there also will thy servant be. (2Sa 15:21)

Isn't this a most comforting thing to say, that in his time of need, these 600 men were prepared to lay down their lives for David?

So it seems that this fits with the title of our Psalm, and also the phrase in verse 2. But what about the babes and sucklings? These were grown men, weren't they?

And David said to Ittai, Go and pass over. And Ittai the Gittite passed over, and all his men, **and all the little ones that were with him**. *(2Sa 15:22)*

So we see that the Gittites came not only with their swords and shields, but also with their wives and children. Was it these children who saw the love and loyalty of their fathers for David, and gave him their own praise and strength too? If so it seems that David was greatly moved by it to pen the words of this song.

Food for thought

Verse 3 - It is a consideration of the greatness of creation which caused David to think about the position of man in the great scheme of things. We should do likewise and realise that despite our insignificance, the creator of all that we can see is concerned for our well being!

Verse 6 - "thou has put all things under his feet" speaks of the supremacy of the risen Christ. See the phrase in 1 Corinthians 15:25 and Ephesians 1:22.

Psalm 9

God makes inquisition for bloodshed

One of the earliest laws God spoke to mankind was about the shedding of blood, or in other words, murder:

> *And surely your blood of your lives will I require; at the hand of every beast will I require it, and at the hand of man; at the hand of every man's brother will I require the life of man. Whoso sheddeth man's blood, by man shall his blood be shed: for in the image of God made he man. (Gen 9:5-6)*

This is a universal law that God holds everyone to. Remember that the flood at Noah's time happened because mankind were murdering each other:

> *The earth also was corrupt before God, and the earth was filled with violence. And God looked upon the earth, and, behold, it was corrupt; for all flesh had corrupted his way upon the earth. And God said unto Noah, The end of all flesh is come before me; for the earth is filled with violence through them; and, behold, I will destroy them with the earth. (Gen 6:11-13)*

Verse 12 of this Psalm uses the same Hebrew word as "require" for "inquisition":

> *When he maketh inquisition for blood, he remembereth them:*
> *he forgetteth not the cry of the humble. (Psa 9:12)*

God would find out the evil being committed and judge that nation for the blood it had shed, and David's army was the means by which that judgement had taken place. Notice also the reason for it is not for vengeance, but to deliver the humble and powerless from murderers:

> *When he maketh inquisition for blood, he remembereth them:*
> *he forgetteth not* **the cry of the humble**. *... For* **the needy** *shall not alway be forgotten: the expectation of* **the poor** *shall not perish for ever. (Psa 9:12, 18)*

Food for thought

Verse 6-7 - Notice the contrast. The Lord will endure "for ever" whilst the enemy will be forgotten. This is the overall picture of redemption. There will come a time when the great enemy – death – is abolished and will be remembered no more. The way in which God deals with the nations is a cameo of His great plan and purpose.

Verse 20 - Man needs to understand that he is "but men". Human nature abrogates to itself notions of invincibility. We must take care that we do not follow in their steps. Our sufficiency is not of ourselves. It is of God.

Psalm 10

Does God allow the poor to be oppressed?

> *Why standest thou afar off, O LORD? why hidest thou thyself in times of trouble? The wicked in his pride doth persecute the poor: let them be taken in the devices that they have imagined. (Psa 10:1-2)*

Why do the wicked oppress the poor while God stands back and appears to allow it? The poor cry out under their oppression, but God doesn't judge the wicked straight away but chooses rather to wait.

The idea that God never judges is, of course, not true. God does judge, and there are plenty of Bible events that show this to be true. It is only the time-frame that is often not what we expect. The book of Jonah explains this enigma in detail. The important thing to come out of this chapter is that no matter how long it takes before God judges an evildoer, in the meantime He will always be a refuge to those who put their trust in Him:

> *Thou hast seen it; for thou beholdest mischief and spite, to requite it with thy hand: the poor committeth himself unto thee; thou*

art the helper of the fatherless. (Psa 10:14)

Exercise: Work out the amount of time God chose to wait before judging the wickedness of Nabal and Manasseh. For Nabal, see 1 Samuel 25:36-39. For Manasseh, see 2 Chronicles 33:9-13 and 2 Kings 34:1-4.

Food for thought

Verse 11 - We can be like the wicked, thinking that God cannot see what we are doing or know what we are thinking. If we realised that He can, then maybe we would find it easier to resist temptation?

Verse 6 - We may, from time to time, wonder whether we are "wicked" when we fall short of what God requires of us. However we must notice that the "wicked" think their evil plans in "their heart" – where they are carefully planned and owned by the wicked. These thoughts are the driving force in their lives. We trust that our (sometimes frequent) shortcomings are a lapse rather than a conscious desire to sin.

Psalm 11

The LORD will deliver the righteous

Notice the logic in this Psalm. If, v7, the LORD loves the righteous and the upright:

> *For the righteous LORD loveth righteousness; his countenance doth behold the upright. (Psa 11:7)*

but, v2, the wicked prepare to shoot at them, and, v4, God sees it:

> *For, lo, the wicked bend their bow, they make ready their arrow upon the string, that they may privily shoot at the upright in heart. ... The LORD is in his holy temple, the LORD'S throne is in heaven: his eyes behold, his eyelids try, the children of men. (Psa 11:2, 4)*

Then, v5, God will hate what they are doing and, v6, He will judge them and deliver the righteous from their hand:

> *The LORD trieth the righteous: but the wicked and him that loveth violence his soul hateth. Upon the wicked he shall rain*

snares, fire and brimstone, and an horrible tempest: this shall be the portion of their cup. (Psa 11:5-6)

Food for thought

Verse 1 - In speaking of "fleeing as a bird", David echoes what he said to Saul – 1Sam 26:20 (partridge) – on one of the occasions when Saul was seeking David's life. So we might conclude that this Psalm has its origins in the time of David's flight from Saul.

Verse 4 - That "the Lord is in His holy temple", we see that He is in control. Habakkuk recognised this and saw that it eventually the whole earth be silent because of it (Habakkuk 2:20)

Psalm 12

Hiding hatred with lying lips

Psalm 12 verse 2 says:

> They speak vanity every one with his neighbour: with flattering lips and with a double heart do they speak. (Psa 12:2)

I wonder if these people were using flattery to hide their hatred? David says in the previous Psalm:

> For, lo, the wicked bend their bow, they make ready their arrow upon the string, that they may privily shoot at the upright in heart. (Psa 11:2)

The word "privily" means "privately". So if these two Psalms are related, this may well have been the case. Proverbs also makes this connection between lying and hatred:

> He that hideth hatred with lying lips, and he that uttereth a slander, is a fool. (Pro 10:18)

We are being instructed to be straightforward in our conversation. If we have a problem with something someone has done, we should perhaps let it out as honestly and gently as we can, lest hiding it away makes it grow into hatred.

Food for thought

Verse 1 - David lamented that "the Godly man" could no longer be found on the earth - in the land of Israel. His despair would be that, given the absence of Godly men, David would struggle to find like minded men and women with whom he could talk. Does our despair about the Godlessness of the world impinge on us because of reduced fellowship or do we stand self righteously simply seeing a Godless world as a further sign that the return of Christ is near?

Verse 6 - It is easy to think that the wicked and their ways do not affect us as we stay away from them. However such a view is wrong, and dangerous. We are all influenced by the things we hear and see. Our children are exposed to it at school and we are when we are at work. The antidote is to appreciate that the "words of the Lord are pure words" (Psa 12:6) and are the only antidote to the evil words and ideas that the world assails us with.

Psalm 13

Singing to the LORD in times of trouble

> *But I have trusted in thy mercy; my heart shall rejoice in thy salvation. I will sing unto the LORD, because he hath dealt bountifully with me. (Psa 13:5-6)*

It must have been difficult for David to rejoice and see that God had dealt bountifully with him. After all, he was being chased by Saul:

> *How long shall I take counsel in my soul, having sorrow in my heart daily? how long shall mine enemy be exalted over me? (Psa 13:2)*

We can see in verse 4 that David felt Saul would overtake him one day; that it was only a matter of time:

> *Lest mine enemy say, I have prevailed against him; and those that trouble me rejoice when I am moved. (Psa 13:4)*

Verse 3 tells us that David knew that would mean his death.

Consider and hear me, O LORD my God: lighten mine eyes, lest I sleep the sleep of death; (Psa 13:3)

Yet David's heart was lifted by faith in his God, who not only comforted him but saved him time and again from his enemy. Let us also remember God's power to answer prayer when we need Him in our own lives and, like David, let's remember to praise Him in our hearts "because He hath dealt bountifully with me".

Food for thought

Verse 4-5 - The injustice of those who oppose us gaining the supremacy is often very hard to bear. David's antidote was to recognise that trust in God is a sufficient comfort for the present trouble.

Verse 6 - Do we ever think to praise God for what He has done for us? Do we think that sort of praise is to be reserved for times when we are together with other believers? Or is it something we might do spontaneously during the day?

Psalm 14

A repeated Psalm

The words of his Psalm are echoed in Psalm 53. What differences can you find between the two? What might the reason be for repeating these words?

Here (**in bold**) are the two main sections that diverge from one another:

> *Have all the workers of iniquity no knowledge? who eat up my people as they eat bread, and call not upon the LORD. There were they in great fear:***for God is in the generation of the righteous. Ye have shamed the counsel of the poor, because the LORD is his refuge.** *Oh that the salvation of Israel were come out of Zion! when the LORD bringeth back the captivity of his people, Jacob shall rejoice, and Israel shall be glad. (Psa 14:4-7)*

> *Have the workers of iniquity no knowledge? who eat up my people as they eat bread: they have not called upon God. There were they in great fear,***where no fear was: for God hath scattered the bones of him that encampeth against thee:**

thou hast put them to shame, because God hath despised them. *Oh that the salvation of Israel were come out of Zion! When God bringeth back the captivity of his people, Jacob shall rejoice, and Israel shall be glad. (Psa 53:4-6)*

Food for thought

Verse 1 - The ruler in Matthew 19:17 should have realised that Jesus would reprove him for his flattery. Psalm 14:1 shows clearly that there is none good.

Verse 4 - Godlessness is something that is in the world and has, therefore, an impact upon us. It is the Godless, not the righteous, who "eat up" God's people. An example is the way in which the Jewish leaders in Luke 20:47 devoured widows' houses.

Psalm 15

What kind of person will dwell with God?

> *LORD, who shall abide in thy tabernacle? who shall dwell in thy holy hill? (Psa 15:1)*

To answer this question, it is a little known fact that there was someone who lived in the tent of God. Look at what is said of Joshua, Moses' servant:

> *And the LORD spake unto Moses face to face, as a man speaketh unto his friend. And he turned again into the camp: but his servant Joshua, the son of Nun, a young man, departed not out of the tabernacle. (Exo 33:11)*

Joshua therefore becomes the example of the character we must adopt in order to dwell with God. Samuel also lived in or around the Tabernacle while he grew up (see 1 Samuel 3:1-15).

Now take a look at the list of character traits in our Psalm:

> *He that walketh uprightly, and worketh righteousness, and speaketh the truth in his heart. He that backbiteth not with*

his tongue, nor doeth evil to his neighbour, nor taketh up a reproach against his neighbour. In whose eyes a vile person is contemned; but he honoureth them that fear the LORD. He that sweareth to his own hurt, and changeth not. He that putteth not out his money to usury, nor taketh reward against the innocent. He that doeth these things shall never be moved. (Psa 15:2-5)

Can you find examples of these in the lives of Joshua and Samuel? These two young men, as well as Jesus himself, show us the way, if we wish to dwell with God.

Food for thought

Verse 1 - David was not asking "who?" because he did not know. Rather he was asking so that he could outline the things that would enable him to inherit the kingdom. We should do likewise. Think about those things which please the father - Philippians 4:8.

Verse 4 - It is wrong to "vow and pay not" (Ecclesiastes 5:4). Our word should be our bond. Our Father is always reliable. If we are to emulate Him we should likewise be reliable, even if our promise is inconvenient to us.

Psalm 16

When is no inheritance a better inheritance?

> *Their sorrows shall be multiplied that hasten after another god: their drink offerings of blood will I not offer, nor take up their names into my lips. (Psa 16:4)*

What a strange thing for David to say. Why would he want to offer someone's blood offering anyway? That was the task of a priest or Levite.

In verse 5 David confesses that God is the portion of his inheritance. He proclaims that he is glad with that portion allotted to him:

> *The LORD is the portion of mine inheritance and of my cup: thou maintainest my lot. The lines are fallen unto me in pleasant places; yea, I have a goodly heritage. (Psa 16:5-6)*

He says the same thing in Psalm 119:

> *Thou art my portion, O LORD: I have said that I would keep thy words. (Psa 119:57)*

This portion can be found described in the book of Numbers, and David may be drawing his words from this:

> *And the LORD spake unto Aaron, Thou shalt have no inheritance in their land, neither shalt thou have any part among them:* ***I am thy part and thine inheritance*** *among the children of Israel. And, behold, I have given the children of Levi all the tenth in Israel for an inheritance, for their service which they serve, even the service of the tabernacle of the congregation. ...it shall be a statute for ever throughout your generations, that among the children of Israel they have no inheritance. But the tithes of the children of Israel, which they offer as an heave offering unto the LORD, I have given to the Levites to inherit: therefore I have said unto them, Among the children of Israel they shall have no inheritance. (Num 18:20-24)*

God had told the children of Levi that they were to have no share in the dividing up of the land. Everyone else was to have a portion, but their portion would be to do the service of the Lord, for which they would receive an adequate living. God said "I am your portion and inheritance".

In saying what he did, David was declaring that he wanted God to be his inheritance. He loved the things of God far more than any temporary inheritance he could gain in this life. By offering himself in this service, he had become the same as a Levite, and as such he saw it as part of his duty to present to God the offerings of the people. This status as a servant to God has always been open to anyone who genuinely desires it, and are chosen by Him according to His foreknowledge. It is gained by separating oneself to Him, as the Levites had done:

> Then Moses stood in the gate of the camp, and said, Who is on the LORD'S side? let him come unto me. And all the sons of Levi gathered themselves together unto him. (Exo 32:26)

Some examples are Melchisedek, Moses, David, Samuel, Samson, and John the Baptist. Are we amongst them?

Food for thought

Verse 7 - In saying "my reins also instruct me in the night season" David is showing us that he meditates upon Scripture. His "reins" here speak of his mind. The mind can only "instruct" if it has been instructed already through reading the Scriptures.

Verse 8 - The word "always" is crucial. We can all, from time to time, set God before our eyes. It is especially easy when we are spending time with fellow believers but ever so hard when we are in the company of those, or those things, which do not have God at the centre. It follows, therefore, that the company of fellow believers is to be preferred above company with those things which do not focus on God. But how easy it is to choose unhelpful situations rather than helpful!

Psalm 17

A prayer when life seems hard

The introductory words in Psalm 17 tell us it is a prayer of David. It is a prayer made in a time of distress, and could provide a pattern for how to pray when you find yourself similarly troubled or anxious.

The first thing we see is that David relinquishes control of the situation to God, by asking Him to pronounce sentence on the situation:

> *[A Prayer of David.] Hear the right, O LORD, attend unto my cry, give ear unto my prayer, that goeth not out of feigned lips.* **Let my sentence come forth from thy presence**; *let thine eyes behold the things that are equal. (Psa 17:1-2)*

In verse 3 he then acknowledges we can't hide anything from Him. In other words, we might as well be totally honest in our prayer:

> *Thou hast proved mine heart; thou hast visited me in the night; thou hast tried me, and shalt find nothing; I am purposed that my mouth shall not transgress. (Psa 17:3)*

In verses 4-5 David asks for God's help in walking the difficult path he has to walk:

> *Concerning the works of men, by the word of thy lips I have kept me from the paths of the destroyer. Hold up my goings in thy paths, that my footsteps slip not. (Psa 17:4-5)*

Then in verses 6-8 he prays for complete protection by God.

> *I have called upon thee, for thou wilt hear me, O God: incline thine ear unto me, and hear my speech. Shew thy marvellous lovingkindness, O thou that savest by thy right hand them which put their trust in thee from those that rise up against them. Keep me as the apple of the eye, hide me under the shadow of thy wings, (Psa 17:6-8)*

This lovely phrase "hide me under the shadow of thy wings" is something David comes back to often in his life, and is taken from the words of his great grandfather, Boaz:

> *The LORD recompense thy work, and a full reward be given thee of the LORD God of Israel, under whose wings thou art come to trust. (Rth 2:12)*

Food for thought

Verse 8 - In asking to be kept as "the apple of the eye" David is asking God to treasure him as much as he does the whole nation (see Deuteronomy 32:10).

Verse 10 - Describing "them" as being "inclosed in their own fat" sounds disgusting. What it is telling us is that "they" are surrounded by their own possessions and as a consequence are proud. It is so easy to trust in our own possessions or wealth as if they save us. Paul taught otherwise – 1Tim 6:17

Psalm 18

How the Bible works: Dual applications

Everything referred to in this Psalm happened to David in 1 Samuel 29 to 31 and in 2 Samuel 1 to 2. Yet these things also happened to Jesus at his death and resurrection. The Psalms are both prophetic (interpreting the future) and explain the mind of the writer at the time. This is one of the ways that the Bible distinguishes itself far above any other writing. We'll take just one example and show how it applies to both Jesus and to David.

See the numbers in square brackets to check how each detail compares to the Psalm.

The Psalm (Psa 18:4-6):

> *The sorrows of death compassed me[1], and the floods of ungodly men made me afraid[2]. The sorrows of hell compassed me about[1]: the snares of death prevented me. In my distress I called upon the Lord, and cried unto my God[3].*

Here is how it applied to Jesus:

> *Then saith he unto them, My soul is exceeding sorrowful, even unto death [1]: tarry ye here, and watch with me. And he went a little further, and fell on his face, and prayed [3]... Then cometh he to his disciples, and saith unto them, Sleep on now, and take your rest: behold, the hour is at hand, and the Son of man is betrayed into the hands of sinners [2] (Matthew 26:38,39,45).*

Here is how it applied in the life of David:

> *Then David and the people that were with him lifted up their voice and wept, until they had no more power to weep [1]. And David was greatly distressed; for the people spake of stoning him [1+2], because the soul of all the people was grieved, every man for his sons and for his daughters: but David encouraged himself in the Lord his God [3] (1Sam 30:4,6).*

This is called "dual application", and the Bible is designed to work in this way. Most things in the Old Testament point forward in some way to Jesus, even when they don't appear (on the surface) to be about him.

Food for thought

Verse 16 - In saying "he drew me out of many waters" David is reflecting on the way in which God took care of Moses (Exodus 2:10) to provide a redeemer for Israel.

Verse 17-18 - We may think of David as a mighty warrior. However he recognises that his enemies were too strong for him. So even though David *was* an exceptional fighting man, he recognised that deliverance came from God. How often do we think that we can overcome some problem by our own strength?

Psalm 19

Presumptuous sins

What do you think the presumptuous sins are in verse 13?

*Keep back thy servant also from **presumptuous sins**; let them not have dominion over me: then shall I be upright, and I shall be innocent from the great transgression. (Psa 19:13)*

If you use a concordance or any Bible software with Strongs or Englishman's search feature, you can find where else in the Bible this particular Hebrew word occurs (Zed).

> **Concordance Results Using KJV**
>
> Strong's Number **H2086** matches the Hebrew זֵד (zed),
> which occurs 13 times in **13** verses in the Hebrew concordance of the KJV
>
> View results using the NASB Hebrew concordance
>
> Psa 19:13 — Keep back thy servant also from presumptuous H2086 *sins*; let them not have dominion over me: then shall I be upright, and I shall be innocent from the great transgression.
>
> Psa 86:14 — O God, the proud H2086 are risen against me, and the assemblies of violent *men* have sought after my soul; and have not set thee before them.
>
> Psa 119:21 — Thou hast rebuked the proud H2086 *that are* cursed, which do err from thy commandments.
>
> Psa 119:51 — The proud H2086 have had me greatly in derision: *yet* have I not declined from thy law.

Screenshot from www.blueletterbible.org

Wherever else it occurs in the old testament it is translated "proud", such as in Isaiah 13:11:

> *And I will punish the world for their evil, and the wicked for their iniquity; and I will cause the arrogancy of the **proud** to cease, and will lay low the haughtiness of the terrible. (Isa 13:11)*

So David is talking about sin where he had proudly assumed he would be forgiven by God, and therefore went ahead and did it anyway. Perhaps that kind of sin is familiar to us too? Paul also talks about it when he asks:

> *"Shall we continue in sin, that grace may abound?"*

(See the answer in Romans 6.)

Food for thought

Verse 8 - "enlightening the eyes" was a request that Ezra made when in captivity (Ezra 9:8). Ezra recognised that enlightenment came from God.

Verse 10 - The Proverb 24:13 makes the point that sweet honey is good to be eaten. However the word of God is more nourishing. The idea of the word of God being sweeter than honey is a point that David makes again – Psa 119:103.

Psalm 20

Chariots of mire

> *The LORD hear thee in the day of trouble; the name of the God of Jacob defend thee; ... Some trust in chariots, and some in horses: but we will remember the name of the LORD our God. (Psa 20:1, 7)*

At least twice in Israel's history God had overcome an army of chariots by miring it in mud (see Exodus 14 and Judges 4). It is by knowledge of God's past miracles combined with faith in His power to repeat them, that David could have confidence. This had to be real and concrete reality for him, because he had been commanded by God not to gather chariots. The nations around him could have as many as they wished:

> *But he shall not multiply horses to himself, nor cause the people to return to Egypt, to the end that he should multiply horses: forasmuch as the LORD hath said unto you, Ye shall henceforth return no more that way. (Deu 17:16)*

Reading the Old Testament will give *us* a similar foundation of knowledge and faith on which to base our actions and our confidence.

Food for thought

The Psalm can be divided up into a call to God (verses 1-4) and a response (verses 5-9) that flows from an appreciation that God will hear the call.

Verse 7 - The problem we have all the time is to learn to trust the God we cannot see, when there are plenty of things we *can* see that we are tempted to put our trust in.

Psalm 21

Saying thank-you for answered prayers

This Psalm records David's praise of God's power by which He had made him King (21:1,13):

> *The king shall joy in thy strength, O LORD; and in thy salvation how greatly shall he rejoice! ... Be thou exalted, LORD, in thine own strength: so will we sing and praise thy power. (Psa 21:1, 13)*

Do we ever look back at how God has brought us through trials, and at all the things He has given us, and praise His power? Looking back on this power in our lives should make us exceedingly glad:

> *For thou hast made him most blessed for ever: thou hast made him exceeding glad with thy countenance. (Psa 21:6)*

And cause us to trust Him even more:

> *For the king trusteth in the LORD, and through the mercy of the most High he shall not be moved. (Psa 21:7)*

Maybe at the start of a new year we should take time out to meditate on last year, how prayers have been answered, count our blessings, and then specifically kneel to offer our thanks and praise?

Food for thought

Verse 2 - David tells us that he had one desire - to dwell in the house of the Lord (Psalm 27:4). This he did when he went and "sat before the Lord" (2 Samuel 7:18). So we can conclude that this Psalm was written after David had brought the ark to Zion.

Verse 11-13 - David, knowing that his enemies are planning evil against him, leaves things in God's hand. God will repay, is David's way of thinking. This is based on the teaching of the law of Moses – see Deuteronomy 32:35.

Psalm 22

All they that see

Though this Psalm is a prophecy about Jesus, it is derived from David's own life. Which event in David's life do you think it could refer to? There are some clues in the text:
Verse 6 - a reproach and despised by the people:

> *But I am a worm, and no man; a reproach of men, and despised of the people.*

Verse 7 - being ridiculed:

> *All they that see me laugh me to scorn: they shoot out the lip, they shake the head...*

Verse 14-15,17 - a serious illness?

> *I am poured out like water, and all my bones are out of joint; my heart is like wax; it is melted in the midst of my bowels. My strength is dried up like a potsherd; and my tongue cleaveth to my jaws; and thou hast brought me into the dust of death*

... I may tell all my bones: they look and stare upon me. (Psa 22:14-15, 17)

Verse 20 - in danger from the sword:

Deliver my soul from the sword; my darling from the power of the dog. (Psa 22:20)

Food for thought

Verse 7 - The laughing to scorn is prophetic of the way that Jesus was treated as can be seen in Mark 5:40.

Verse 8 - This verse was on the lips of Jesus' enemies when he was crucified (see Matthew 27:43). Little did they know that by their sneering words they were fulfilling elements of a Psalm which Jesus took great comfort from.

Psalm 23

What was David scared of in the Valley of Death?

Have you ever read the famous Psalm 23 and noticed that verse 4 just doesn't make any sense? If I were to make a list of comforting things, a rod and staff certainly wouldn't feature! So what did David mean?

> *Yea, though I walk through the valley of the shadow of death, I will fear no evil: for thou art with me; thy rod and thy staff they comfort me. (Psa 23:4)*

In the book of Jeremiah a rod and staff are used to describe the strength and glory of Moab:

> *The calamity of Moab is near to come, and his affliction hasteth fast. All ye that are about him, bemoan him; and all ye that know his name, say, How is the strong staff broken, and the beautiful rod! (Jer 48:16-17)*

In Isaiah 10:24 it's the might of Assyria:

> *Therefore thus saith the Lord GOD of hosts, O my people that dwellest in Zion, be not afraid of the Assyrian: he shall smite thee with a rod, and shall lift up his staff against thee, after the manner of Egypt.*

In Isaiah 10:5 we learn that Assyria were in fact God's rod and staff with which He caused His judgements to come on the nations:

> *O Assyrian, the rod of mine anger, and the staff in their hand is mine indignation.*

So following the Bible usage of the phrase "rod and staff" it would appear David is saying 'knowing about Your might and power (in battle) comforts me.'

This would fit in perfectly with the context of the Psalm in verses 4-5:

> *Yea, though I walk through the valley of the shadow of death, **I will fear no evil**: for thou art with me; thy rod and thy staff they comfort me. Thou preparest a table before me in **the presence of mine enemies**: thou anointest my head with oil; my cup runneth over. (Psa 23:4-5)*

Food for thought

Verse 2 - The lying down in green pastures is seen in the feeding of the 5,000 in Mark 6:39.

Verse 4 - In saying 'I will fear no evil' David is reflecting on the promise made to Joshua and Caleb (Psalm 91:10).

Psalm 24

Righteousness by faith or by effort?

In Psalm 24 there is a blessing promised to those who do something specific. First, here's the blessing:

> He shall receive the blessing from the LORD, and righteousness from the God of his salvation. (Psa 24:5)

It seems to me that the blessing here is righteousness itself.

In the preceding verse is the list of things someone has to do to receive this blessing:

> He that hath clean hands, and a pure heart; who hath not lifted up his soul unto vanity, nor sworn deceitfully. (Psa 24:4)

Note that righteousness here is not included in the list of things to do. Think about that. Righteousness is not something you do.

Perhaps the rich young ruler had it wrong when he said to Jesus:

> ... Good Master, what good thing shall I do, that I may have eternal life? (Mat 19:16)

If he had read the Psalm he would have understood that eternal life is not inherited by good works (righteousness), but righteousness is a gift.

Jesus himself had said it a few chapters earlier:

Blessed are the meek: for they shall inherit the earth. (Mat 5:5)

This meekness is typified perhaps in the Psalm, which talks about having clean hands, a pure heart, not swearing deceitfully and not lifting up (becoming proud) the heart.

Food for thought

Verse 1 - In saying "the earth is the Lord's" David is reminded of what Pharaoh had to learn during the plagues – see Exodus 9:29.

Verse 4 - The "pure heart" is not the heart of a man who never sins. Rather it is the heart of a man who has God and His purpose at the centre of his life. Whilst the natural heart is 'deceitful' – Jeremiah 17:9 – the faithful servant has his focus on the things of the kingdom – Matthew 6:21.

Psalm 25

Learning God's way during trials

Have you noticed that in the middle of the trouble David is describing here, his focus is that God might teach him?
v4 -teach me thy paths.
v5 -lead me in thy truth, and teach me.
v8 -therefore will He teach sinners in the way.
v9 -The meek will He guide in judgment: and the meek will He teach His way.
v12 - What man is he that feareth the Lord? him shall He teach in the way that He shall choose.
v14 - He will shew them His covenant

Food for thought

Verses 2, 3, 20 - Being 'ashamed' is a major concern of David in this Psalm. His concern is that those who trust God should not be ashamed. One presumes he means not ashamed of God. Thus David is concerned about God's ability to save him, in terms of what that might say about God's power to others.

Verse 6 - In asking God to remember His tender mercies and loving kindness David is appealing to God's character as shown in Exodus 34:6.

Psalm 26

How could David love God's house before it was ever built?

In giving due praise to God, and in an expression of his desire to serve the Lord, David offers this statement:

> LORD, I have loved the habitation of thy house, and the place where thine honour dwelleth. (Psa 26:8)

With the power of hindsight we could say that, of all people in Scripture, David was the best placed to sincerely praise God in this way. He was after all the man who prepared for the building of God's temple. But hang on a minute, how could David love the house of God if it wasn't there yet? How could David say he loved the place where God's glory dwelt, when that glory did not appear until the time of his son?

> And it came to pass, when the priests were come out of the holy place, that the cloud filled the house of the LORD, So that the priests could not stand to minister because of the cloud: for

the glory of the LORD had filled the house of the LORD. (1Ki 8:10-11)

The answer is found in Psalm 27 - and we will pick up the thread in the next chapter.

I've done it!

Have you noticed the similarity between this Psalm and Psalm 1?

> *Blessed is the man that walketh not in the counsel of the ungodly, nor standeth in the way of sinners, nor sitteth in the seat of the scornful. But his delight is in the law of the LORD; and in his law doth he meditate day and night. (Psa 1:1-2)*
>
> *I have not sat with vain persons, neither will I go in with dissemblers. I have hated the congregation of evil doers; and will not sit with the wicked...For thy lovingkindness is before mine eyes: and I have walked in thy truth. (Psa 26:4-5,3)*

In Psalm 1 he is explaining what someone needs to do to be blessed. In this Psalm he is saying he has done it.

Food for thought

Verse 3 - David, recognising God's 'loving-kindness' in his life, is moved to walk 'in thy truth'. How often does our appreciation of what God has done for us cause us to modify our actions?

Verse 6 - In saying that he has washed his hands in innocency David is saying that he is not guilty of the blood of any dead man, appealing to the language of Deuteronomy 21:6 where the elders of the city declare their position about a dead body found near to their city.

Psalm 27

Dwelling in God's house

In Psalm 27 David continues his theme from Psalm 26. Here we see in v4-5 that he sought to dwell in the house of God:

> One thing have I desired of the LORD, that will I seek after; that I may dwell in the house of the LORD all the days of my life, to behold the beauty of the LORD, and to enquire in his temple. For in the time of trouble he shall hide me in his pavilion: in the secret of his tabernacle shall he hide me; he shall set me up upon a rock. (Psa 27:4-5)

In verse 5 he declares that God will hide him in that place, and save him from trouble. But since when has God's temple been a refuge? And how could David take refuge in an un-built house! What's more, in 26:8 we read that he *had* been there, and he had loved inhabiting it:

> LORD, I have loved the habitation of thy house, and the place where thine honour dwelleth. (Psa 26:8)

In 1Chron 17:1-8 we have the request of David that he might build God a house. The reply of God was, effectively 'haven't I always been with you anyway?'

> *Now therefore thus shalt thou say unto my servant David, Thus saith the LORD of hosts, I took thee from the sheepcote, even from following the sheep, that thou shouldest be ruler over my people Israel: And I have been with thee whithersoever thou hast walked, and have cut off all thine enemies from before thee, and have made thee a name like the name of the great men that are in the earth. (1Ch 17:7-8)*

The comment on this in Acts 7:46-49 is "the Most High does not dwell in temples made with hands". We, like David, can forget that God's concern is not with material things, but with spiritual. God's dwelling place is in heavenly places, and not in earthly. So how had David dwelt with God? Every time David was in trouble, he put his trust in God. His faith and hope was in God. *In* God. David's salvation was in God, and none other. His trust was in heavenly things and not earthly. David lived in faith. He lived *in* faith *in* God. Notice the italics?

A reading of 27:1-6 shows us that whenever David was in trouble, he fled for refuge in God. It is this that is defined as dwelling in the house of the LORD. God himself is a refuge. Our trust in Him is a concrete and solid thing. The bunker or tower that is God, is more real, more impenetrable, more un-assailable than anything earthly. When one trusts in the Lord, that safety is so sure and so complete that one is actually in a heavenly tower, house, or habitation:

> *For in the time of trouble he shall hide me in his pavilion: in the secret of his tabernacle shall he hide me; he shall set me up*

> upon a rock. (Psa 27:5)

It is by faith that one enters into that house. And as it turns out, David was not talking about the temple Solomon built at all.

Food for thought

Verse 1 - David's confidence, against the difficulties he faced in life is amazing. Or maybe his confidence is because he has experienced so many difficulties and been delivered from them. Do we see the difficulties we experience in life and our continued survival as an evidence of God's care for us?

Verse 5 - Being hid in a time of trouble is echoed later by the prophet – Zephaniah 2:3.

Psalm 28

God will be a shield to those who trust in Him

In verse 7 David calls the LORD his strength and shield:

> *The LORD is my strength and my shield; my heart trusted in him, and I am helped: therefore my heart greatly rejoiceth; and with my song will I praise him. (Psa 28:7)*

God had helped him when David trusted in Him, and that was what David described as his shield.

God revealed Himself to Abraham in the same way:

> *After these things the word of the LORD came unto Abram in a vision, saying, Fear not, Abram: I am thy shield, and thy exceeding great reward. (Gen 15:1)*

So this is clearly a part of God's work with those who trust in Him. In contrast, the shield of Saul, David's enemy, was no use to him for protection:

> *Ye mountains of Gilboa, let there be no dew, neither let there be*

rain, upon you, nor fields of offerings: for there the shield of the mighty is vilely cast away, the shield of Saul, as though he had not been anointed with oil. (2Sa 1:21)

So we can contrast someone who put their trust in God (David) with someone who put their trust in shield and spear, forgetting God (Saul). The result was that God became the shield of the one trusting in Him, and for the other, even his physical shield failed him.

Food for thought

Verse 1 - David's worry is that his fellowship with his God might be destroyed – that he might not hear God's word. Whilst our Father does not speak directly to us He does speak to us through His word. Failing to 'listen' to Him by reading the Bible will have the consequence that we may lose contact with Him completely.

Verse 3 - "draw me not away" shows David shared the sentiments in the Lord's Prayer (see Matthew 6:13). Is this our prayer? Or do we think that we have the strength to resist temptations, and so do not ask God to direct our steps away from temptation?

Psalm 29

The voice of the LORD upon the waters

The voice of the LORD is upon the waters: the God of glory thundereth: the LORD is upon many waters. (Psa 29:3)

There are two other specific occasions in Scripture where the voice of the LORD was upon the waters. Firstly when He created the world the Bible says this:

And the earth was without form, and void; and darkness was upon the face of the deep. And the Spirit of God moved upon the face of the waters. And God said, Let there be light: and there was light. (Gen 1:2-3)

Secondly, when the LORD brought Israel out of Egypt there is a comment in the Psalms about the red sea crossing:

The waters saw thee, O God, the waters saw thee; they were afraid: the depths also were troubled. The clouds poured out water: the skies sent out a sound: thine arrows also went abroad. The voice of thy thunder was in the heaven: the lightnings

> *lightened the world: the earth trembled and shook. Thy way is in the sea, and thy path in the great waters, and thy footsteps are not known. Thou leddest thy people like a flock by the hand of Moses and Aaron. (Psa 77:16-20)*

So in this third occasion, the Psalmist may have been calling to mind these two acts of God, both of which showed His great power and glory.

But which Old Testament event does our Psalm refer to? The clue is in verse 10:

> *The LORD sitteth upon **the flood**; yea, the LORD sitteth King for ever. (Psa 29:10)*

It was the flood at the time of Noah where God once again covered the earth with sea, as He had done at creation, and as He had partially done at the red sea crossing. The context of the Psalm makes sense in this light, for example the sweeping away of forests as the great Tsunami of water hit them:

> *The voice of the LORD breaketh the cedars; yea, the LORD breaketh the cedars of Lebanon. (Psa 29:5)*

Food for thought

Verse 3 - "The voice of the Lord" here and in the subsequent verses is seen to be the motivator in much of creation. We might have thought that God's creative work finished at the end of day 6 of creation. During creation He spoke and it was done (Genesis 1). We are caused to see in this Psalm that God's work never ceases in keeping His creation working.

Verse 10 - There are seven times in the Psalm when we read of "the voice of the Lord". These occurences correlate to the seven instances in Genesis that we are told of God speaking to Noah (Gen 6:13, 22, 7:5,9, 8:15,9:8,17). This, along with verse 10 containing the only occurence of the word "flood" outside Genesis, helps us to understand that the Psalm is focussing on the flood in the days of Noah.

Psalm 30

David and Job: brothers in affliction

Psalm 30 echoes the message of the book of Job. Here we read how David praised God after God allowed him to be afflicted for a time, then saved him. David called out to God and He listened. David then likens his affliction to a single night after which the morning comes. You can see further similarities between Job and the Psalm here:

> And **in my prosperity** I said, I shall never **be moved (shaken)**. (Psa 30:6)
> **I was at ease**, but he hath broken me asunder: he hath also taken me by my neck, and **shaken me to pieces**, and set me up for his mark. (Job 16:12)

and:

> LORD, by thy favour thou hast made my mountain to stand strong: **thou didst hide thy face**, and I was troubled. (Psa 30:7)
> Wherefore **hidest thou thy face**, and holdest me for thine enemy? (Job 13:24)

How many other similarities can you find?

Food for thought

Verse 1 - Does our worship of God stem from a deep seated recognition of the deliverance from sin and death that we have benefited from? The contrast of our position before and after accepting Jesus is emphasised in Romans 3:23-24. Until we appreciate what sinfulness does to our relationship with God, we cannot appreciate the joy of forgiveness.

Verse 9-11 - David had mourned as he fled from Saul. Now, when he brought the ark to Zion he "danced before the Lord" (2Samuel 6:21). Reflecting on his deliverance from Saul, he sees life as an opportunity to praise his God.

Psalm 31

Prophecy of Jesus or for Jesus?

We tend to think of the Psalms as prophecies of Jesus, and that's true as far as it goes.

However, a more helpful way to think of it is that God provided David's life as an example for Jesus to follow. David's thoughts are written down as a way for Jesus to read, internalise, understand, and then carry out his life's mission. They were a platform on which Jesus could build his life.

This Psalm is a good example. Here's how it may have worked. When Jesus studied this Psalm, he would then work out what events in David's life it applied to. Then he meditated about how God had rescued David from those troubles, how God had responded to David's particular plea for help. Then he tucked away the thoughts, sentiments and emotions contained in the Psalm for mental fuel when he faced similar circumstances.

In verse 3 he may have noticed that the word "fortress", used several times in the Psalm, reminded him of David's time in the fortress while fleeing Saul:

Bow down thine ear to me; deliver me speedily: be thou my

> *strong rock, for an **house of defence** to save me. For thou art **my rock and my fortress**; therefore for thy name's sake lead me, and guide me. (Psa 31:2-3)*
>
> *And he brought them before the king of Moab: and they dwelt with him all the while that David was in **the hold**. And the prophet Gad said unto David, Abide not in **the hold**; depart, and get thee into the land of Judah. Then David departed, and came into the forest of Hareth. (1Sa 22:4-5)*

It was here in this situation of great distress that David learned to put his life totally in his Father's hands, and as a result penned the words that would become the very words in Jesus' mind as he faced his greatest distress — the cross.

> *Into thine hand I commit my spirit: thou hast redeemed me, O LORD God of truth. (Psa 31:5)*
>
> *And when Jesus had cried with a loud voice, he said, Father, into thy hands I commend my spirit: and having said thus, he gave up the ghost. (Luk 23:46)*

Like Jesus, we can do the same. If we study the scriptures now, the thoughts we develop will give us fuel for later. Jesus taught this principle with the parable of the wise virgins storing up oil (Matt 25:1-13).

Food for thought

Verse 8 - Have you ever felt trapped by your circumstances? David did, but was delivered by his God and rejoiced in that deliverance from Saul and all his enemies (see 2 Samuel 22:20).

Verse 13 - The taking counsel against David was prophetic of the trial of Jesus (see Matt 27:1), so we might conclude that David's emotion of "fear" in this verse was also the emotion of Jesus at that time.

Psalm 32

The joy of forgiveness

Here is one way of looking at this Psalm and what it means. The number in brackets is the respective verse number:

> There is no-one happier than a sinner who doesn't get their just deserts (1). As long as you're honest about your sin (2). If not, and you try to hide it, God just turns on the thumb screws till you can't stand it (3-4). But when you finally come out in the open and confess, He forgives it all (5). That's why everyone who understands God's way of working, prays to Him straight away (6). And rather than hiding from Him like Adam and Eve, they hide with Him and are delivered (7). Let's accept this teaching, and not be stubborn with God when we sin, so He has to force us to our knees to confess (9). That kind of attitude brings so much heartache. But those who trust that God will forgive, have so much joy in that forgiveness (10-11).

David's thoughts on Noah's deliverance

> *For this shall every one that is godly pray unto thee in a time when thou mayest be found: surely in the floods of great waters they shall not come nigh unto him. (Psa 32:6)*

Perhaps this is a comment on the flood of Genesis. It's not hard to imagine songs of deliverance being sung on that boat, helping to remind the passengers that the deadly waters encompassing them were in fact the means of their deliverance :

> *Thou art my hiding place; thou shalt preserve me from trouble; thou shalt compass me about with songs of deliverance. Selah. (Psa 32:7)*

Verse 7 is telling us that God Himself is an Ark of refuge. It means that deliverance, like that of Noah, is available to us, no matter where we are or when. We can access it by prayer (see verse 6) and trust:

> *Many sorrows shall be to the wicked: but he that trusteth in the LORD, mercy shall compass him about. (Psa 32:10)*

Food for thought

Verse 1 - David is 'the man' whose sins have been forgiven after he had committed adultery with Bathsheba. Paul says (Romans 4:5-8) that we are blessed in the same way in that our sins can be forgiven also. Thus David's repentance and God's subsequent forgiveness forms a pattern of forgiveness to those who repent and believe.

Verse 3 - The 'roaring' of this verse echoes David's despair as voiced

PSALM 32

in Psalms 22:1.

Psalm 33

God knows the hearts of kings and princes

We are used to seeing the lives of rulers and politicians paraded in front of us in newspapers, television, and on the internet. We recognise their faces and, perhaps, almost think we know them personally. But what we see is just a facade for the cameras. God, however, sees the real men and women, from the inside. And what does He do with this knowledge? He brings about events for them that move them for His own purposes:

> *The LORD looketh from heaven; he beholdeth all the sons of men. From the place of his habitation he looketh upon all the inhabitants of the earth. He fashioneth their hearts alike; he considereth all their works. (Psa 33:13-15)*

And by manipulating the private thoughts of each country's decision makers, he can, if He wishes, render all their best laid plans useless:

> *The LORD bringeth the counsel of the heathen to nought: he maketh the devices of the people of none effect. The counsel of the LORD standeth for ever, the thoughts of his heart to all*

generations. (Psa 33:10-11)

Maybe the best examples of this are in the book of Daniel where each successive emperor is moved by God in one way or another, either by dream, Daniel's influence, or direct intervention.

So when we next look at a famous person, let's recognise that they may be, in some way unknown to them, carrying out God's purpose.

Food for thought

Verse 6 - Both Peter (2 Peter 3:5) and Paul (Hebrews 11:3) quote this verse. The involvement of God in creation is the bedrock of our faith. If we cannot accept that God did create the universe as Genesis describes then we cannot move on to believe anything else of the gospel. Creation – God's work – is one of the pillars upon which we build the rest of the gospel.

Verse 3-4 - Do we praise God because of a realisation that His word – the Scriptures – are "right" – that is inspired and infallible?

Psalm 34

Taste and see that the LORD is good

This Psalm makes solid observations about God's care for those who love Him, but sets this treasure in the frame of our afflictions:

> Many are the afflictions of the righteous: but the LORD delivereth him out of them all. (Psa 34:19)

So what we have is a realistic picture of life for those who fear God. We can look back at David's life to see how these promises are worked out, in particular how he was fed time and time again...

> O fear the LORD, ye his saints: for there is no want to them that fear him. The young lions do lack, and suffer hunger: but they that seek the LORD shall not want any good thing. (Psa 34:9-10)

...delivered from troubles...

> This poor man cried, and the LORD heard him, and saved him

> out of all his troubles. The angel of the LORD encampeth round about them that fear him, and delivereth them. ... The righteous cry, and the LORD heareth, and delivereth them out of all their troubles. (Psa 34:6-7, 17)

...and even rescued out of his heartbreak:

> The LORD is nigh unto them that are of a broken heart; and saveth such as be of a contrite spirit. (Psa 34:18)

If we take time to read (taste) these Bible accounts and match them to the Psalms, then apply them when we are next in trouble, we will both **taste** and **see** that the LORD is good:

> O taste and see that the LORD is good: blessed is the man that trusteth in him. (Psa 34:8)

Unfortunately, if we leave out the tasting part, we might miss the seeing too.

Answered prayer builds faith

Other Bible references to "taste" refer to the word of God, but in this Psalm the word refers to the experience of answered prayer. Praying in time of trouble (v6) and being delivered as a result (v7) is the personal evidence we all need to prove to us that God is good. These experiences produce faith, or "trust" as this Psalm has it. Both faith and an appreciation of God's goodness are needed in order for us to be acceptable to God, and so we can see why a certain amount of trouble can be an important catalyst for godliness in our lives.

But without faith it is impossible to please him: for he that cometh to God must believe that he is, and that he is a rewarder of them that diligently seek him. (Heb 11:6)

Food for thought

Title - The title of this Psalm shows us why the Psalm was written. There is a change in focus of the Psalm at verse 11 where David moves from speaking about how God has worked in his own life, to talking about instructing his "children". These children, in the first instance are the 400 who were with him in the cave (see 1 Samuel 22), which is the next event recorded after he escaped from Gath.

Verse 19 - Paul, in 2 Timothy 3:11-12, uses these reassuring words of David to encourage Timothy.

Psalm 35

Joab's net

Draw out also the spear, and stop the way against them that persecute me: say unto my soul, I am thy salvation. (Psa 35:3)

I wonder whether David was thinking about what happened to Asahel, brother to Joab?

And Asahel pursued after Abner; and in going he turned not to the right hand nor to the left from following Abner. ... And Abner said to him, Turn thee aside to thy right hand or to thy left, and lay thee hold on one of the young men, and take thee his armour. But Asahel would not turn aside from following of him. ... Howbeit he refused to turn aside: wherefore Abner with the hinder end of the spear smote him under the fifth rib, that the spear came out behind him; and he fell down there, and died in the same place: and it came to pass, that as many as came to the place where Asahel fell down and died stood still. (2Sa 2:19, 21, 23).

We see that Abner drew out the spear, and the dead body of Asahel stopped the way so that all the soldiers who came that way stood still.

Joab was furious at this killing, and took his revenge years later, killing Abner by striking him "under the fifth rib" as he had smote his brother:

> *And when Abner was returned to Hebron, Joab took him aside in the gate to speak with him quietly, and* **smote him there under the fifth rib**, *that he died, for the blood of Asahel his brother. (2Sa 3:27)*

Another link in this Psalm to Joab is in verse 16:

> *With hypocritical mockers in feasts, they gnashed upon me with their teeth. (Psa 35:16)*

This feasting sounds similar to when Joab forsook David and made a feast to proclaim Adonijah king instead of David. Think of the mocking of David that would have gone on there:

> *For he is gone down this day, and hath slain oxen and fat cattle and sheep in abundance, and hath called all the king's sons, and the captains of the host, and Abiathar the priest; and, behold, they eat and drink before him, and say, God save king Adonijah. (1Ki 1:25)*

Do these links to Joab potentially tell us that the mystery man mentioned in verse 8 is Joab?

> *Let destruction come upon him at unawares; and let his net that he hath hid catch himself: into that very destruction let him fall. (Psa 35:8)*

Food for thought

Verse 1 - In asking God to "plead my cause" David, even though he was the powerful king of Israel, does not rely on his kingly status but rather leaves injustices in God's hands. If king David did that, we have a wonderful example to copy when we feel we are wronged.

Verse 19 - This verse is actually prophetic of the Lord Jesus in John 15:25. From the Psalm we see that Jesus was distressed by the evil thoughts and actions of his opponents.

Psalm 36

How God rewards the humble with wisdom

In this chapter I want to demonstrate in a practical way that God rewards the humble with their request, and keeps knowledge from the proud. This chapter is a little longer than the others.

We're looking at Psalm 36 and our request is "please let us understand it". If you want to, you can pray that prayer now, or think it in the quiet of your mind, and then proceed. If you find that uncomfortable then just read on - that's ok too.

Do we understand the Psalm?

Let's look at the Psalm. It looks the same as any Psalm, and when we read it we feel that some general point is being made but we don't know what. If we are humble, we will say "I don't understand this". If we're proud, we pass over the meaning of the Psalm, feeling that we do understand, and that in some way having merely read it, we will benefit from it. This is the point of departure between the proud and humble. The humble say "I don't understand"; the proud say "I understand" (when they really don't). We could therefore also say that the humble is being honest, and the proud dishonest. Pride stops us from understanding the meaning of the word of God.

The next step after this humble admission is to reflect on the nature of God. Is he unable to give us a coherent message? No, we're told He is wise beyond anything we can understand. He knows the end from the beginning. Job (one of the wisest men who ever lived) said:

> *With him is wisdom and strength, he hath counsel and understanding. (Job 12:13)*

So God is able to explain this Psalm to us.

Next, is God *willing* to help us, or does He want to leave us to work it all out for ourselves on our own? The answer is that Jesus said "ask and it shall be given". Jesus likens God to a Father who is only too willing to share good things with His children if we ask Him (see Matt 7:7-11).

So God is able, and God is willing, and the means by which we will obtain good things is that we just ask, then seek. We've asked already, so now we're ready to seek.

Looking for signposts

Let's look at the Psalm for anything that stands out. If we really believe that God wants to help us, then we must believe that He has left something easy for humble people to grasp onto. God must have left some signpost or marker telling us how to interpret the Psalm. We don't need to look far. In the heading to the Psalm we see something odd:

> *To the chief Musician, A Psalm of David, the servant of the Lord.*

(By the way, headings to Psalms are part of Scripture itself. Headings that the English translators put in are not part of Scripture, and they use a different font or text style in your Bible.)

David calls himself "the servant of the Lord" at the start of this Psalm. This is our signpost because the Psalms don't usually start with this. To draw an analogy, in a room full of people, if only one person wears a uniform, you assume they are significant in some way. In a room full of uniformed people, you may assume the one plain clothed person is significant. So it is with Scripture. You can only tell if something is particularly significant by looking at the context.

Where does the signpost lead?

Where else does this phrase "servant of the Lord" appear? In other words, where does the signpost point us to? Type this phrase into a Bible search program (such as biblegateway.com) and look through the results. Soon enough we see that in the book of Joshua, Moses is called "the servant of the Lord" many times over. We can therefore assume that this is where the signpost is pointing. No doubt the wise scholars of Scripture would turn their noses up at this simple method, but then again, God doesn't reveal His secrets to them - He reveals them to the humble:

> *But on this one will I look: On him who is poor and of a contrite spirit, And who trembles at My word. (Isa 66:2)*

If we tremble at His word, it means we fear and respect the power of it. In our case, we so respect God, that we presume He will lead us to the answer simply and without the convoluted arguments of worldly wisdom.

Having received this signpost we now see that the Psalm is linked to

Moses in some way. Both David and Moses were called the "servant of the Lord", and David is choosing to make this connection by headlining the Psalm with this title.

Reading the Psalm again with fresh perspective

Read through the Psalm again with Moses in mind. Try to think of the words of the Psalm as if Moses were penning the words. What is there that could apply to Moses? Perhaps the following sentence might stand out:

Let not the foot of pride come against me, and let not the hand of the wicked remove me. (Psa 36:11)

Was there a time when proud men wanted to bring Moses down and remove him from his role of leadership? Looking elsewhere in the Psalm we can see the same theme:

For he flattereth himself in his own eyes, until his iniquity be found to be hateful. The words of his mouth are iniquity and deceit: he hath left off to be wise, and to do good. He deviseth mischief upon his bed; he setteth himself in a way that is not good; he abhorreth not evil. (Psa 36:2-4)

It's clear from the wording that David is talking of a specific person isn't he? So we can ask, was there a specific man that wanted to replace Moses?

Well, yes there certainly was! Depending on the amount of time we may have spent reading the Bible in our lives until now, we will either come to the name "Korah" straight away, or we may have needed to flick through the Bible to remind ourselves of the life of Moses, or we may have been stuck and needed to ask someone. All of these are valid ways to go about it.

Whichever path we took, we have arrived at one man - Korah.

The key: Scripture comes in pairs

Every part of Scripture comes as a pair. It has a passage elsewhere in Scripture that partners with it. And it is the partners that illuminate each other. The animals came two by two into the ark; why? because with a male and a female conception is possible, and therefore the pairs could be fruitful. If we wish the Scripture to bear fruit it must be paired with other Scripture, but that pairing must be God provided not contrived by us or else it will be barren. Reading the Psalm with Korah in mind, and reading about the Korah uprising (Numbers 16) with the Psalm in mind, will reveal some things both about David and about the life of Moses that we could not know otherwise.

The big question that rises to the surface is: "was there someone in David's life who acted in the same way as Korah?"

We can be confident God really wants us to make this connection, because there are many other details that also link the two partner passages together, for example compare verse 12 with Numbers 16:32-33,

> *And the earth opened her mouth, and swallowed them up, and their houses, and all the men that appertained unto Korah, and all their goods. They, and all that appertained to them, went down alive into the pit, and the earth closed upon them: and they perished from among the congregation. (Num 16:32-33)*

> *There are the workers of iniquity fallen: they are cast down, and shall not be able to rise. (Psa 36:12)*

Food for thought

Verse 2 - Flattering yourself in your own eyes is comparing yourself with yourself – see 2 Corinthians 10:12.

Verse 4 - The "wicked" differs from the Godly. The "wicked" thinks about evil on his bed. The Godly, on the other hand, think of God's work (see Psalm 63:6).

Psalm 37

What it means to be a child of God

Those who trust God don't just swim through life never falling. But the promise is when they do they will not fall headlong because God is holding their hand.

> *Though he fall, he shall not be utterly cast down: for the LORD upholdeth him with his hand. (Psa 37:24)*

It's a parent and child picture. And this is how Jesus led his life.

> *I the LORD have called thee in righteousness, and will hold thine hand, and will keep thee, and give thee for a covenant of the people, for a light of the Gentiles; (Isa 42:6)*

Food for thought

Verse 7 - Humanly speaking the strong inherit - or more correctly take by force - what they want. The "meek" on the other hand leave things in God's hands knowing that He is mightier than them all.

Verse 39 - Israel thought it was their own righteousness which counted before God (see Romans 10:3), but here the Psalmist shows it is God's righteousness which brings salvation. Paul explains that this is so in Romans 3:25-26.

Psalm 38

Can illness come because of sin?

There are many reasons why we or our loved ones go through illness. We can find ourselves questioning why these things happen. In this Psalm we have an example of where illness came upon David because of his grave sin in committing adultery and murder.

> A Psalm of David, to bring to remembrance. *O LORD, rebuke me not in thy wrath: neither chasten me in thy hot displeasure. For thine arrows stick fast in me, and thy hand presseth me sore. There is no soundness in my flesh because of thine anger; neither is there any rest in my bones because of my sin. For mine iniquities are gone over mine head: as an heavy burden they are too heavy for me. My wounds stink and are corrupt because of my foolishness.* (Psa 38:1-5)

David had sinned gravely. Not only that, but he had not yet come to repentance, and therefore was undergoing God's chastening. This manifested itself in what appears to be the same illness that Hezekiah bore. See for example the sore/boil in verse 5 and 11, and compare the account of Hezekiah's illness:

> *For Isaiah had said, Let them take a lump of figs, and lay it for a plaister upon the boil, and he shall recover. (Isa 38:21)*

If it is the same illness, then David was actually going to die from it, as Hezekiah was, before God healed him:

> *In those days was Hezekiah sick unto death. And Isaiah the prophet the son of Amoz came unto him, and said unto him, Thus saith the LORD, Set thine house in order: for thou shalt die, and not live. (Isa 38:1)*

Deuteronomy 28 confirms this, and makes the link between this un-healable boil and the sin that causes it:

> *But it shall come to pass, if thou wilt not hearken unto the voice of the LORD thy God, to observe to do all his commandments and his statutes which I command thee this day; that all these curses shall come upon thee, and overtake thee ... The LORD will smite thee with the botch of Egypt, and with the emerods, and with the scab, and with the itch, whereof thou canst not be healed. (Deu 28:15, 27)*

Note the wording "thou canst not be healed". This is what both Hezekiah and David had. It's mentioned again later in the chapter to hammer home the point that these boils would be incurable:

> *The LORD shall smite thee in the knees, and in the legs, with **a sore botch that cannot be healed**, from the sole of thy foot unto the top of thy head. (Deu 28:35)*

God forced David to come to terms with his sin, to repent and to call upon God as the only one who could forgive and heal. It is possible that this was also the same illness as King Asa who, unlike David and Hezekiah, did not repent and call on God. Instead he sought advice from doctors:

> *And Asa in the thirty and ninth year of his reign was diseased in his feet, until his disease was exceeding great: yet in his disease he sought not to the LORD, but to the physicians. (2Ch 16:12)*

So the Scripture is clear that there is a time when grave sin can lead to illness, and these illnesses may well be brought upon the sinner by God. This is nothing to be fearful about, as we can see God's mercy in forgiving and healing both David and Hezekiah. Even more so for us, since we have a high priest dwelling in the presence of God in heaven, who is able to mediate on our behalf when we ask for forgiveness:

> *Seeing then that we have a great high priest, that is passed into the heavens, Jesus the Son of God, let us hold fast our profession. For we have not an high priest which cannot be touched with the feeling of our infirmities; but was in all points tempted like as we are, yet without sin. Let us therefore come boldly unto the throne of grace, that we may obtain mercy, and find grace to help in time of need. (Heb 4:14-16)*

Food for thought

Verse 2 - In speaking of God's "arrows" David is speaking like Job who lamented God's involvement in his life (see Job 6:4).

Verse 4 - We need to get to the state of mind where we feel that our iniquities are too great for us. It is all too easy to think that by sheer effort we will be able to overcome our sins. This cannot be, though we should try. Jesus died for us because we cannot save ourselves.

Psalm 39

"I am consumed by the blow of thine hand"

> *Remove thy stroke away from me: I am consumed by the blow of thine hand. When thou with rebukes dost correct man for iniquity, thou makest his beauty to consume away like a moth: surely every man is vanity. Selah. (Psa 39:10-11)*

These astonishing words of David's agony show clearly that David is suffering a terrible illness as a result of his sin. And David knows it is God that has brought this upon him:

> *I was dumb, I opened not my mouth;* **because thou didst it.** *(Psa 39:9)*

David is however humble enough to see that it is only God who can save him:

> *And now, Lord, what wait I for? my hope is in thee. (Psa 39:7)*

God is our Father and He will chasten us where necessary, for:

... what son is he whom the father chasteneth not? (Heb 12:7)

Rather it is that chastening, and our response to it, that confirms our parentage.

Food for thought

Verse 1 - It is not always wise to speak even if one has something to say. Ecclesiastes 3:7 teaches this principle. James also draws on the idea of controlling our tongue in James 1:26

Verse 9 - The silence of the one who was rebuked because the rebuke was of God, was, ultimately, Jesus (see Isaiah 53:7).

Verse 10 - David realised his chastening was at the hand of God in that he asked God to remove his "stroke" Rather like the way that Isaiah 53:4 speaks of Jesus' suffering being "of God".

Psalm 40

How the Psalms explain the Parables and sayings of Jesus

Many of the Lord's parables are derived from these Psalms. For example, the parable of the talents, in part, is seen in verse 10:

> *I have not hid thy righteousness within my heart; I have declared thy faithfulness and thy salvation: I have not concealed thy lovingkindness and thy truth from the great congregation. (Psa 40:10)*

We can see here the opposite of the man who hid the gift of God:

> *Then he which had received the one talent came and said, Lord, I knew thee that thou art an hard man, reaping where thou hast not sown, and gathering where thou hast not strawed: And I was afraid, and went and hid thy talent in the earth: lo, there thou hast that is thine. His lord answered and said unto him, Thou wicked and slothful servant... (Mat 25:24-26)*

So in this context we can see that the Lord Jesus probably meant the talents to refer to the forgiveness of God, in receipt of which we ought to gratefully proclaim God's goodness to others, as we see in the rest of the Psalm:

> *And he hath put a new song in my mouth, even praise unto our God: many shall see it, and fear, and shall trust in the LORD. ... Many, O LORD my God, are thy wonderful works which thou hast done, and thy thoughts which are to us-ward: they cannot be reckoned up in order unto thee: if I would declare and speak of them, they are more than can be numbered. ... Let all those that seek thee rejoice and be glad in thee: let such as love thy salvation say continually, The LORD be magnified. (Psa 40:3, 5, 16)*

Another example of a parable is in verse 12:

> *For innumerable evils have compassed me about:* **mine iniquities have taken hold upon me***, so that I am not able to look up;* **they are more than the hairs of mine head:** *therefore my heart faileth me. ... But I am poor and needy; yet* **the Lord thinketh upon me:** *thou art my help and my deliverer; make no tarrying, O my God. (Psa 40:12, 17)*

Notice the wording in bold text, and see how similar it is to the following parable.

> *Are not two sparrows sold for a farthing? and one of them shall not fall on the ground without your Father. But* **the very hairs of your head are all numbered.** *Fear ye not therefore, ye are of more value than many sparrows. (Mat 10:29-31)*

The parable is talking about God's ability to know everything about you, even to count the hairs on your head. The Psalm adds the extra texture to this, by explaining that God even knows all our sins, but yet is willing to forgive them all.

Food for thought

Verse 2 - The "horrible pit" and the "miry clay" represent the depths David was in when he realised his sin. Is this how we view our unforgiven sins?

Verse 14 - Those that devised evil against Jesus and came to capture him in the garden of Gethsemane, fell backwards (see John 18:6) – as David prayed his enemies would do.

Psalm 41

The friend who lifted his heel against David

> *Yea, mine own familiar friend, in whom I trusted, which did eat of my bread, hath lifted up his heel against me. (Psa 41:9)*

Who is the "close friend" who turned against David? How would we go about finding the answer?

Well, there are two particular details contained in this verse, and it stands to reason that God has supplied these to give us the man's identity.

1. He ate David's bread,
2. He "lifted up his heel".

If you type "eat bread" into a Bible search engine, and look at passages in the life of David, you will be taken to Mephibosheth:

> *And David said unto him, Fear not: for I will surely shew thee kindness for Jonathan thy father's sake, and will restore thee all the land of Saul thy father; and* **thou shalt eat bread at my table continually.** *(2Sa 9:7)*

The phrase "eat bread at David's table" is used 5 times on this occasion. The other distinguishing feature about him is that he was lame "in both his feet":

> *So Mephibosheth dwelt in Jerusalem: for he did eat continually at the king's table; and was lame on both his feet. (2Sa 9:13)*

Notice this specifically says "feet", which is possibly why David uses the specific phrase "lifted up his heel".

So Mephibosheth may be the man we're looking for. This man stayed behind in Jerusalem when David fled during perhaps his greatest time of trouble. It is clear that David was deeply upset at Mephibosheth, and didn't have any patience with the explanation he gave afterwards:

> *And the king said unto him, Why speakest thou any more of thy matters? I have said, Thou and Ziba divide the land. (2Sa 19:29)*

Whether or not Mephibosheth betrayed David, it is clear from this Psalm that David was very upset during the time that he thought he had been betrayed, and bitterly disappointed. This is understandable, because Mephibosheth was the last remaining relative of his greatest friend, Jonathan, and perhaps he had been able to see an echo of that friendship when he was with him?

Food for thought

Verse 7 - David, doubtless, did not realise what was going on in secret in the court when he saw others conferring together. It was not until afterwards did he appreciate the intrigue that had been plotted against him.

Verse 1 - Considering the poor was a fundamental requirement of the law of Moses. See Deuteronomy 15:7-11.

II

Psalms 42-72

Psalm 42

Why have You forgotten me?

> *O my God, my soul is cast down within me: therefore will I remember thee from the land of Jordan, and of the Hermonites, from the hill Mizar. (Psa 42:6)*

Mount Hermon (the Hermonites being mentioned here) is the source of the Jordan river. David appears to remember visiting there and seeing the sheer quantity of water gushing out of the water springs:

> *Deep calleth unto deep at the noise of thy waterspouts: all thy waves and thy billows are gone over me. (Psa 42:7)*

How is it then that he now feels so thirsty? At the start of the Psalm he explains that it is God's deliverance that he seeks, like a deer panting for water:

> To the chief Musician, Maschil, for the sons of Korah. *As the hart panteth after the water brooks, so panteth my soul after thee, O God. My soul thirsteth for God, for the living God:*

> *when shall I come and appear before God? (Psa 42:1-2)*

He likens God's ability to save to the source of that river, yet for so many days he has cried out for it and found no water - or in other words, no deliverance:

> *I will say unto God my rock,* **Why hast thou forgotten me?** *why go I mourning because of the oppression of the enemy? (Psa 42:9)*

David even thought God had forgotten him.

But God doesn't forget, and cannot forget. Sometimes God doesn't save immediately but allows us to wait. This is because He sometimes has other plans than what is immediately apparent to us, or perhaps He wants to see how we'll react.

The children of Israel panted for water as they walked through the wilderness. On this occasion God decided to wait so that He could see how they would react:

> *So Moses brought Israel from the Red sea, and they went out into the wilderness of Shur; and they went three days in the wilderness, and found no water. ... And the people murmured against Moses, saying, What shall we drink? And he cried unto the LORD; and the LORD shewed him a tree, which when he had cast into the waters, the waters were made sweet: there he made for them a statute and an ordinance, and* **there he proved them.** *(Exo 15:22, 24-25)*

The lesson here is that we need to be patient, and rather than complain as the children of Israel did, we should take David's example and pour out our prayers continually to God while we wait for His deliverance. Ironically, if the children of Israel had walked on a little longer, they would have found a place prepared with twelve watering holes, one for each tribe!

> *And they came to Elim, where were twelve wells of water, and threescore and ten palm trees: and they encamped there by the waters. (Exo 15:27)*

Food for thought

Verse 11 - Having realised that he was downcast David did some self analysis. He questioned himself asking why he should be so cast down given that God has been so good to him. Surely a lesson for us here.

Verses 5, 6, 11 - Three times the Psalmist talks about being 'cast down'. Three times in the Garden of Gethsemane, Jesus prayed to his Father (Matthew 26:39-44).

Psalm 43

Thy Holy Hill

It is possible at this time that David had not yet discovered God's "holy hill" upon which he would later prepare for the site of the temple. So he asked to be shown its location.

> O send out thy light and thy truth: let them lead me; let them bring me unto thy holy hill, and to thy tabernacles. (Psa 43:3)

God answered this prayer, and that site was eventually made known to him by the angel in the account recorded in 1 Chronicles 21:15-30.

Around that time it was impossible for David to worship at the altar of God, and therefore he was seeking an alternative place. Compare the context of following to see how the two passages are linked:

> At that time when David saw that the LORD had answered him in the threshingfloor of Ornan the **Jebusite**, then he sacrificed there. For the**tabernacle** of the LORD, which Moses made in the wilderness, and **the altar of the burnt offering**, were at that season in the high place at Gibeon. But David could not go before it to enquire of God: for he was afraid because of the

sword of the angel of the LORD. (1Ch 21:28-30)
*O send out thy light and thy truth: let them lead me; let them bring me unto **thy holy hill**, and to thy **tabernacles**. Then will I go unto **the altar of God**, unto God my exceeding joy: yea, upon the harp will I praise thee, O God my God. (Psa 43:3-4)*

The detail missing in the Chronicles passage is the hill, but it does say that it was where the Jebusite lived:

And David and all Israel went to Jerusalem, which is Jebus; where the Jebusites were, the inhabitants of the land. (1Ch 11:4)

And Jerusalem, or more specifically, Zion, is a place on a hill.

Yet have I set my king upon my holy hill of Zion. (Psa 2:6)

Food for thought

Verse 1 - David's pleading is a prayer because of the uprising of Absalom. In speaking of the nation as being 'ungodly' David recognised that the people, by following Absalom, had turned against the king of God's appointing. It was not simply a personal affront to David when Absalom rose to take the throne. It was rebellion against God.

Psalm 44

Standing aside from rebellion

> *All this is come upon us; yet have we not forgotten thee, neither have we dealt falsely in thy covenant. Our heart is not turned back, neither have our steps declined from thy way. (Psa 44:17-18)*

The claim in these two verses is simply not true of Israel. They *had* forgotten God, they *had* dealt falsely with His covenant, and they *had* departed from His paths. So this Psalm is obviously personal to the writers, not dealing with Israel as a whole. The writers of the Psalm were going against the flow.

The title of this Psalm reads "a contemplation of the sons of Korah". Korah had been the instigator of the rebellion against Moses (see Numbers 16), and his punishment was unusual to say the least:

> *So they gat up from the tabernacle of Korah, Dathan, and Abiram, on every side: and Dathan and Abiram came out, and stood in the door of their tents, and their wives, and their sons, and their little children. And Moses said, Hereby ye shall know that the LORD hath sent me to do all these works; for I have*

not done them of mine own mind. ... And the earth opened her mouth, and swallowed them up, and their houses, and all the men that appertained unto Korah, and all their goods. They, and all that appertained to them, went down alive into the pit, and the earth closed upon them: and they perished from among the congregation. (Num 16:27-28, 32-33)

Notice here that while the families of Dathan and Abiram are mentioned, the family of Korah is not. So it seems that his family did the sensible thing and got away from their wicked father at Moses' warning:

And he spake unto the congregation, saying, Depart, I pray you, from the tents of these wicked men, and touch nothing of theirs, lest ye be consumed in all their sins. (Num 16:26)

So Korah's sons refused to be led by his example, standing aside from his sin, and thus their lives were spared. It is wonderful to see that their faithfulness continued through generations, culminating in the inclusion of these, their Psalms, in the Holy Bible.

The lesson from this Psalm is that God will always look after us if we stand aside from evil, even though at times that may be extremely difficult, especially if we are going against peer group pressure or even our own family.

*And Jesus answered and said, Verily I say unto you, There is no man that hath left house, or brethren, or sisters, or **father, or mother**, or wife, or children, or lands, for my sake, and the gospel's, But he shall receive an hundredfold now in this time, houses, and brethren, and sisters, and mothers, and children, and lands, with persecutions; and in the world to come eternal* *life. (Mark 10:29-30)*

Food for thought

Verses 1, 4 - Because David had 'heard' about God's work for Israel in the past he was able to say 'Thou art my God'. He could put confidence in a God who had already demonstrated His faithfulness.

Verse 6 - In asserting that he will not trust in his own weapons David differs from all of us. Generally we feel we can sort out our own problems. David was willing to leave things in God's hand. A powerful lesson for us.

Psalm 45

Like father like son

It is clear from the words of this Psalm that this is a prophecy relating to Jesus. So why is Jesus called "God" in verses 6-7?

> *Thy throne, O God, is for ever and ever: the sceptre of thy kingdom is a right sceptre. Thou lovest righteousness, and hatest wickedness: therefore God, thy God, hath anointed thee with the oil of gladness above thy fellows. (Psa 45:6-7)*

We might think this is a complex question, relating to the trinity, and therefore a mystery. But as always, God has given us the answer in His Scripture — and there is nothing mysterious about it. If we simply look at the context of where this passage is quoted in the New Testament (Hebrews 1:6), the book starts with the following:

> **God**, *who at sundry times and in divers manners spake in time past unto the fathers by the prophets, Hath in these last days* **spoken unto us by his Son**, *whom he hath appointed heir of all things, by whom also he made the worlds; Who* **being the brightness of his glory, and the express image of his person**,

and upholding all things by the word of his power, when he had by himself purged our sins, sat down on the right hand of the Majesty on high. (Heb 1:1-3)

So quite simply: the son is the very image of his Father, and just as you or I can be called by the name of our parent, Jesus could be called by the name of his. And just as you or I can remind others of our parents by our looks, mannerisms, and way of speech, so could Jesus.

Food for thought

Verse 2 - "grace is poured into thy lips" is seen to have its fulfilment in Jesus (Luke 4:22).

Verse 7 - Hating wickedness contrasts powerfully with Psalm 52:3, speaking of Doeg the Edomite (see 1 Samuel 22). Doeg is so different from David.

Psalm 46

Taking refuge in God

Therefore will not we fear, though the earth be removed, and though the mountains be carried into the midst of the sea; (Psa 46:2)

In the Gospel of Mark, Jesus quotes this Psalm:

And Jesus answering saith unto them, Have faith in God. For verily I say unto you, That whosoever shall say unto this mountain, Be thou removed, and be thou cast into the sea; and shall not doubt in his heart, but shall believe that those things which he saith shall come to pass; he shall have whatsoever he saith. Therefore I say unto you, What things soever ye desire, when ye pray, believe that ye receive them, and ye shall have them. (Mar 11:22-24)

He explains that by prayer we can move mountains. So we can see, by implication, that the refuge spoken of in the Psalm is obtainable by prayer:

To the chief Musician for the sons of Korah, A Song upon Alamoth. *God is our refuge and strength, a very present help in trouble. ... The LORD of hosts is with us; the God of Jacob is our refuge. Selah. ... The LORD of hosts is with us; the God of Jacob is our refuge. Selah. (Psa 46:1, 7, 11)*

Food for thought

Verse 1 - That God is the refuge of the Psalmist is a recurring theme in Scripture. However it is so hard, in times of trouble, to realise that God is our refuge. It is so easy to try to rely on our own strength. The situations where we have to rely on God are part of His training plan that we might learn that we cannot rely on ourselves but must rely on Him.

Verse 6 - The raging heathen and kingdoms moved, explains verses 2-3. The Psalm, when speaking of the elements, is using them as metaphors for the nations.

Verse 9 - God will make wars to cease when Jesus rules from Jerusalem (see Isaiah 2:4).

Psalm 47

Sing praises with understanding

What do you think verse 7 is teaching us when it says "sing ye praises with understanding?"

> Sing praises to God, sing praises: sing praises unto our King, sing praises. For God is the King of all the earth: sing ye praises with understanding. (Psa 47:6-7)

Perhaps we would think that singing praises is easy enough: learn some words, a melody, and then sing along together.

But this verse seems to suggest there's more to it than that. In the first verse of the Psalm we have a further suggestion about how to go about offering praise:

> ...O clap your hands, all ye people; shout unto God **with the voice of triumph**. (Psa 47:1)

So they are told to shout, to clap, and to sing with the voice of triumph. This sounds like the kind of song sung after a victory doesn't it? The next verses confirm this for us:

> *For the LORD most high is terrible; he is a great King over all the earth.* **He shall subdue the people under us, and the nations under our feet.** *He shall choose our inheritance for us, the excellency of Jacob whom he loved. Selah. (Psa 47:2-4)*

But the thing about a victory song is that it's only joyful for the victors. The defeated do not sing with the voice of triumph.

So on a very simple level here is an explanation as to why we must sing praises with understanding. We have to be in a position where the words we are singing apply to us, and in order to do that, we have to first understand them.

Food for thought

Verse 1-4 - The Psalmist sings of the victory that God has provided, hence (v5) God has gone up with a shout. This language is quoted by Paul to speak of the victory we shall gain at the return of Christ (see 1Thess 4:16).

Verse 8 - If we truly believe that it is God that reigns over everyone, then we will have confidence that He will work out everything according to His purpose. We will not be troubled when world events seem to be deteriorating. It is difficult to appreciate the distress felt by those who do not have this assurance.

Psalm 48

How the Psalms interpret Old Testament events

Beautiful for situation, the joy of the whole earth, is mount Zion, on the sides of the north, the city of the great King. (Psa 48:2)

This Psalm is about the City of David, Zion, so why does it suddenly mention ships of Tarshish? Zion is not on the coast!

Thou breakest the ships of Tarshish with an east wind. (Psa 48:7)

The verse appears to refer to two events in the Old Testament. First, Solomon had built ships to sail to Tarshish, and it was from there that he appears to have gained a lot of his wealth:

For the king had at sea a navy of Tharshish with the navy of Hiram: once in three years came the navy of Tharshish, bringing gold, and silver, ivory, and apes, and peacocks. (1Ki 10:22)

Notice that Solomon was King in Jerusalem at the time, so we could surmise that the "great king" in verse 2 refers to him. The second occasion is when King Jehoshaphat built a fleet of ships to try to repeat Solomon's achievement:

> *And he joined himself with him to make ships to go to Tarshish: and they made the ships in Eziongeber. Then Eliezer the son of Dodavah of Mareshah prophesied against Jehoshaphat, saying, Because thou hast joined thyself with Ahaziah, the LORD hath broken thy works. And the ships were broken, that they were not able to go to Tarshish. (2Ch 20:36-37)*

So the Psalm is obviously a commentary on that particular event. We learn from the Psalm how God achieved the destruction of those ships (with an East wind), and we learn from 2 Chronicles when and where the event took place. Most events in the Psalms can be linked in that way.

Also the lesson of the Psalm is hidden until we discovered this link. The lesson of the Psalm is that Zion, the city of God, is beautiful and sufficient in itself. Jehoshaphat should not have tried to ally himself with another King, especially not one that had rejected God. The lesson for us is that we are to learn of, and embrace, the holiness of God while rejecting all outside wisdom. The Psalm directs us to mark well what we have been given, to delight in it, rather than seeking to gain enlightenment elsewhere. Ironically, Jehoshaphat learned his lesson and remained faithful, whereas Solomon did not.

Food for thought

Verse 2 - The joyful description of Jerusalem is contrasted by Jeremiah (see Lamentations 2:15) with how he saw it after the Babylonians had taken Judah captive. However its fortunes will be restored when the Lord Jesus returns.

Verse 8 - In this turbulent world where change is all around us. When the future in the Middle East looks so uncertain, it is most reassuring to know that God has a plan for Jerusalem which no man can change.

Psalm 49

Understanding

Verse 4 links this Psalm with chapter 1 of Proverbs:

> *My mouth shall speak of wisdom; and the meditation of my heart shall be of **understanding**. I will incline mine ear to a parable: I will open my **dark saying** upon the harp. (Psa 49:3-4)*

The theme of understanding "dark sayings" is the same as that in the introduction to Proverbs, where it explains the reason for the book:

> *A wise man will hear, and will increase learning; and a man of **understanding** shall attain unto wise counsels: To understand a proverb, and the interpretation; the words of the wise, and their **dark sayings**. (Pro 1:5-6)*

If we compare the contexts of the two chapters closely we find the reason for Solomon's main statement in Proverbs:

> *Wisdom is the principal thing; therefore get wisdom: and with*

*all thy getting get **understanding**. (Pro 4:7)*

The reason is, understanding elevates us above the animals, and in the end saves us from their fate. This is what David leads up to later in our Psalm:

> *Like sheep they are laid in the grave; death shall feed on them; and the upright shall have dominion over them in the morning; and their beauty shall consume in the grave from their dwelling. ... Man that is in honour, and **understandeth not**, is like the beasts that perish. (Psa 49:14, 20)*

Can we pay our own ransom?

Look at the way the words redeem/ransom are used in this chapter:

> *They that trust in their wealth, and boast themselves in the multitude of their riches; None of them can by any means **redeem** his brother, nor give to God a **ransom** for him: (For the **redemption** of their soul is precious, and it ceaseth for ever.) (Psa 49:6-8)*

Here we get the rich man who can never pay the whole ransom for his life. If he were to live forever, it seems like he would have to go on paying forever:

> *(For the redemption of their soul is precious, and it ceaseth for ever:) That he should still live for ever, and not see corruption. (Psa 49:8-9)*

So the Psalmist concludes how pointless it is to try and pay God, or to earn salvation. Instead he realises that God will freely pay the whole ransom:

> But **God will redeem** my soul from the power of the grave: for he shall receive me. Selah. (Psa 49:15)

This idea of the folly of paying your own ransom, can be seen in many of Jesus' teachings.

> *Verily I say unto thee, Thou shalt by no means come out thence, till thou hast paid the uttermost farthing. (Mat 5:26)*
> *When thou goest with thine adversary to the magistrate, as thou art in the way, give diligence that thou mayest be delivered from him; lest he hale thee to the judge, and the judge deliver thee to the officer, and the officer cast thee into prison. I tell thee, thou shalt not depart thence, till thou hast paid the very last mite. (Luk 12:58-59)*

Food for thought

Verse 4 - David's expression about "parable" and "dark saying" is seen again in Psalm 78:2

Verse 9 - Those who trust in their own wealth are like Adam and Eve - on hearing the words of the serpent they thought that they would be able to live for ever by their own strength and cunning. Of course, just like Adam and Eve, they will die. It is (v15) God who is the redeemer.

Psalm 50

Judge not, that ye be not judged

Jesus' New Testament teachings can all be derived from the Old Testament. It was his daily bread and where he got his inspiration.

For example, there are two parties in this chapter who go to court to accuse someone. In verses 4-7 God accuses His people:

> He shall call to the heavens from above, and to the earth, that he may judge his people. Gather my saints together unto me; those that have made a covenant with me by sacrifice. And the heavens shall declare his righteousness: for God is judge himself. Selah. Hear, O my people, and I will speak; O Israel, and I will testify against thee: I am God, even thy God. (Psa 50:4-7)

And the reason for his accusation is that they are an unmerciful people, condemning even their own family members (v19-20):

> Thou givest thy mouth to evil, and thy tongue frameth deceit. Thou sittest and speakest against thy brother; thou slanderest thine own mother's son. (Psa 50:19-20)

Was Jesus thinking about this Psalm when he said "Judge not, that you be not judged"? (Matt 7:1-3). Can you think of any other teaching he may have derived from this Psalm?

> *Judge not, that ye be not judged. For with what judgment ye judge, ye shall be judged: and with what measure ye mete, it shall be measured to you again. And why beholdest thou the mote that is in thy brother's eye, but considerest not the beam that is in thine own eye? (Mat 7:1-3)*

Food for thought

Verse 2 - Whilst Zion was "the perfection of beauty", that beauty was spoiled (Lamentations 2:15) through the unwillingness of Israel to appreciate the message of this Psalm.

Verse 17 - That the people cast God's words behind them is an idea which Nehemiah picks up – Neh 9:26.

Psalm 51

What comes after forgiveness?

> To the chief Musician, A Psalm of David, when Nathan the prophet came unto him, after he had gone in to Bathsheba. *Have mercy upon me, O God, according to thy lovingkindness: according unto the multitude of thy tender mercies blot out my transgressions. (Psa 51:1)*

In saying "have mercy on me" this Psalm looks like it's a prayer for forgiveness. But try reading the Psalm through with the following in mind. Does it change the way you view it?

The heading of the Psalm says "when Nathan the Prophet came unto him," so when David wrote the Psalm, God *had already pronounced forgiveness* for his sin against Uriah and Bathsheba:

> And David said unto Nathan, I have sinned against the LORD. And Nathan said unto David, The LORD also hath put away thy sin; thou shalt not die. *(2Sa 12:13)*

So if the Psalm is not a request for forgiveness of sin, what is it about? And what can we learn about our own prayers from this? (Clue: List all David's specific requests in this Psalm, and see what he is really asking for.)

Food for thought

Verse 1 - The idea of sins being blotted out is taken up by Paul in Colossians 2:14.

Verse 7 - "purge" "hyssop" "wash" are words drawn from the details of the Red Heifer – Numbers 19:1-9. That animal is a pattern of the one-off sacrifice of Jesus.

Psalm 52

The price of fighting against God

Doeg the Edomite lied to bring about the death of God's priests, as recorded in 1 Samuel chapters 21 and 22. Here in Psalm 52, David prophecies that God would visit punishment on him:

> *God shall likewise destroy thee for ever, he shall take thee away, and pluck thee out of thy dwelling place, and root thee out of the land of the living. Selah. (Psa 52:5)*

Did this come to pass when David became King and fought against the Edomites? The Bible records that David cut off every male from Edom:

> *For it came to pass, when David was in Edom, and Joab the captain of the host was gone up to bury the slain, after he had smitten every male in Edom; (For six months did Joab remain there with all Israel, until he had cut off every male in Edom:) (1Ki 11:15-16)*

This would certainly fit, as the verse talks about the complete rooting out of his family line forever. God picks up the thread in Jeremiah 49, where He prophecies of the total overthrow of Edom's dwelling place like the destruction of Sodom and Gomorrah:

> *Also Edom shall be a desolation: every one that goeth by it shall be astonished, and shall hiss at all the plagues thereof. As in the overthrow of Sodom and Gomorrah and the neighbour cities thereof, saith the LORD, no man shall abide there, neither shall a son of man dwell in it. (Jer 49:17-18)*

Food for thought

Verses 1-5 - This Psalm which relates to Doeg killing all the priests at Nob reads more like a personal letter sent to Doeg - notice the pronouns :1 thyself :2 thy :3 thou :4 Thou :5 thee. One wonders if it was ever read by Doeg.

Verse 8 - The idea of a faithful man being like an olive tree is seen elsewhere, for example Psalm 128:3.

Psalm 53

The days of Noah repeated

Whatever situation David is faced with when writing Psalm 53, it is reminding him of the hopeless situation at the time of Noah. For example, see the similarity between the Genesis account and this Psalm in the following verses:

> And God looked upon the earth, and, behold, it was corrupt; for all flesh had corrupted his way upon the earth. (Gen 6:12)

> God looked down from heaven upon the children of men, to see if there were any that did understand, that did seek God. Every one of them is gone back: they are altogether become filthy; there is none that doeth good, no, not one. (Psa 53:2-3)

There are some clues as to what David was bothered about:

> Have the workers of iniquity no knowledge? who eat up my people as they eat bread: they have not called upon God. (Psa 53:4)

The only time in the Bible where we have anyone eating anyone else is when the spies of Israel come to Canaan and see the giants:

> *And they brought up an evil report of the land which they had searched unto the children of Israel, saying, The land, through which we have gone to search it, is a land that eateth up the inhabitants thereof; and all the people that we saw in it are men of a great stature. (Num 13:32)*

So when David says "every one of them is gone back," he is referring to the backsliding of Israel; gradually adopting the idolatrous practices of the nations that inhabited the land before them. This is the link with Noah - for it was in those days that the giants also seem to have been the greatest agents for the descent into evil of that society:

> *There were giants in the earth in those days; and also after that, when the sons of God came in unto the daughters of men, and they bare children to them, the same became mighty men which were of old, men of renown. And GOD saw that the wickedness of man was great in the earth, and that every imagination of the thoughts of his heart was only evil continually. (Gen 6:4-5)*

Food for thought

Verse 1 - Scripturally a "fool" is someone who does not listen to sound instruction. See Proverbs 10:8.

Verse 2 - That God "looked down" is rather like the way that He looked and then went down to Sodom (Gen 18:21).

Psalm 54

Betrayed by strangers

In the heading to the Psalm we read this interesting snippet:

> *To the chief Musician on Neginoth, Maschil, A Psalm of David, when the Ziphims came and said to Saul, Doth not David hide himself with us? (Psa 54:1)*

It's referring 1Sam 23:14-24 and 1Sam 26, a major event in David's life. His betrayal by these strangers for no apparent reason was a source of great distress:

> *For strangers are risen up against me, and oppressors seek after my soul: they have not set God before them. Selah. (Psa 54:3)*

We can see clearly that with a little searching, each Psalm can be put into its context. The text in Samuel tells us what happened, and the Psalm tells us what David was thinking and adds in extra detail. This is one of the great keys to Bible understanding: every passage in Scripture has its counterpart elsewhere that illuminates it.

Note that most headings in your Bible are inserted by the Bible translators to aid us in navigating the text, but in Psalms the headings are part of the original Bible text itself — they are as much part of the inspired word of God as the rest.

Food for thought

Verse 2 - David's own countrymen were his betrayers - Ziph was in the inheritance of Judah (Josh 15:24). Even though betrayed by his own tribe David still seeks for God to bring deliverance (v2). He left things in God's hands rather than seeking justice himself.

Verse 6 - David, in saying that his sacrifice will be freely given, highlights an attitude which should be ours in all aspects of our worship of God. It should be willing, not because we feel obligated – 2Cor 9:7.

Psalm 55

Condemn not, that ye be not condemned

We probably can't think of too many worse sins than adultery and murder. This is what King David did, and as a direct result he garnered the hatred of one of his own close acquaintances. Psalm 55:21 describes this man's inner feelings:

> *The words of his mouth were smoother than butter, but* **war was in his heart**: *his words were softer than oil, yet were they drawn swords. (Psa 55:21)*

We might think that it was right for this man to hate David. He had seen David commit a great sin, and he wanted justice to be done. He viewed David as a transgressor. Yet in the next verse (v22) David describes himself as righteous. How is this possible?

> *Cast thy burden upon the LORD, and he shall sustain thee: he shall never suffer the righteous to be moved. (Psa 55:22)*

And in verse 23, he describes how God would protect him from his enemy. Yet the way he describes his enemy actually also describes what David had done himself!

> *But thou, O God, shalt bring them down into the pit of destruction:* **bloody and deceitful men** *shall not live out half their days; but I will trust in thee. (Psa 55:23)*

The big lesson here is that God forgives those who seek forgiveness; and when He forgives it is total. David was now a righteous man again. God had removed his sin so that it didn't even exist any more. This man, however, still remembered, and therefore he faced the wrath of God for the actions he had taken against David.

We need to be careful when retaining memories of another's sins. How are we to know if God has already taken that sin away? If we judge another person in our hearts, we can set ourselves up in direct opposition to God, who will go to any lengths to vindicate His righteous (forgiven) servants. This is why Jesus commanded "judge not, that you be not judged."

> *Be ye therefore merciful, as your Father also is merciful. Judge not, and ye shall not be judged: condemn not, and ye shall not be condemned: forgive, and ye shall be forgiven. (Luk 6:36-37)*

Food for thought

Verse 7 - Going to the wilderness is exactly what David did when he fled from Absalom – 2 Samuel 17:16.

Verses 13-14 - The word "Maschil" in the title, meaning "instruction", indicates that this Psalm is meant for instruction. It speaks of David's distress when his friend, probably Ahithophel, betrayed him. We must take care that we do not let our friends down. The closer we are to someone the greater is the pain if we fail them.

Psalm 56

The Giants of Gath

> To the chief Musician upon Jonathelemrechokim, Michtam of David, when the Philistines took him in Gath. *Be merciful unto me, O God: for man would swallow me up; he fighting daily oppresseth me. (Psa 56:1)*

Referring to the title of the Psalm, it seems unbelievable that David would flee from Saul into the hands of the Philistines in Gath. But such was his fear of the 7ft giant (King Saul) that he failed to take into account the giants dwelling in Gath. We read in 2 Samuel 21:22 that at least four giants had been born to Goliath, the giant of Gath:

> *These four were born to the giant in Gath, and fell by the hand of David, and by the hand of his servants. (2Sa 21:22)*

We should not underestimate the threat that these men posed to David, remembering that David had, after all, killed their father. This threat rose above the threat of Saul when David heard them quote the song which had been sung after his victory over Goliath.

> *And it came to pass as they came, when David was returned from the slaughter of the Philistine, that the women came out of all cities of Israel, singing and dancing, to meet king Saul, with tabrets, with joy, and with instruments of musick. And the women answered one another as they played, and said, Saul hath slain his thousands, and David his ten thousands. (1Sa 18:6-7)*
>
> *And the servants of Achish said unto him, Is not this David the king of the land? did they not sing one to another of him in dances, saying, Saul hath slain his thousands, and David his ten thousands? (1Sa 21:11)*

David realised that, whilst the king of Gath had no animosity toward him, those giants certainly did. We read at the end of David's life that these giants had dogged him until the end, so much so that at the death of the last one, he penned the song recorded in 2Sam 22:

> *And David spake unto the LORD the words of this song in the day that the LORD had delivered him out of the hand of all his enemies, and out of the hand of Saul: (2Sa 22:1)*

In 22:49 he writes "You also lift me up above those who rise against me." And thus ended his struggle with men who towered over him.

What happened to David in Gath?

When we take Psalm 56 in the context of that song, we can derive an account of what may have happened in Gath. See 2Sam 22:17-19 and compare it with Psa 56:5-6 to see how they conspired to turn king Achish against him:

> *He sent from above, he took me; he drew me out of many waters; He delivered me from my strong enemy, and from them that hated me: for they were too strong for me. They prevented me in the day of my calamity: but the LORD was my stay. (2Sa 22:17-19)*
>
> *Every day they wrest my words: all their thoughts are against me for evil. They gather themselves together, they hide themselves, they mark my steps, when they wait for my soul. (Psa 56:5-6)*

And finally, they confronted him openly as we have seen in 1Sam 21:11.

Food for thought

Title - This Psalm is to be seen as complementing Psalm 34. David was going to Gath when, as this Psalm's title says, David was captured by the Philistines. David is then arrayed before Achish. Psalm 34 talks of that incident.

Verse 4 - So we learn where David's confidence was. He learnt, as Psalm 34 shows, that he could not work out his problem and had to rely on his God. It took David time to get to the position where he trusted God rather than seeking his own solution. Going down to Gath had been *his* solution. We too need to learn to rely on God. Over time we will find out that cannot rely on our own wisdom and planning.

Psalm 57

Resisting fierce opposition

> To the chief Musician, Altaschith, Michtam of David, **when he fled from Saul in the cave.** *Be merciful unto me, O God, be merciful unto me: for my soul trusteth in thee: yea, in the shadow of thy wings will I make my refuge, until these calamities be overpast. (Psa 57:1)*

The title for Psalm 57 says "when [David] fled from Saul into the cave" and the margin refers to the occasion of 1Sam 22:1 but this doesn't seem to fit the Psalm.

> *David therefore departed thence, and escaped to the cave Adullam: and when his brethren and all his father's house heard it, they went down thither to him. (1Sa 22:1)*

At this time David wasn't in danger from his own men. It does however seem to fit with 1Sam 24 where his men urged him to kill Saul. Verse 7 tells us he had to restrain them, and v4 and 10 that they applied pressure to him to do it:

> *So **David stayed his servants with these words, and suffered them not to rise against Saul.** But Saul rose up out of the cave, and went on his way. ... Behold, this day thine eyes have seen how that the LORD had delivered thee to day into mine hand in the cave: and **some bade me kill thee:** but mine eye spared thee; and I said, I will not put forth mine hand against my lord; for he is the LORD'S anointed. (1Sa 24:7, 10)*

This appears from the extra information we're given in the Psalm to have been a make or break moment for David, whose men were "set on fire" and "their tongues a sharp sword" (v4):

> *My soul is among lions: and I lie even among them that are set on fire, even the sons of men, whose teeth are spears and arrows, and their tongue a sharp sword. (Psa 57:4)*

They thought the answer to all their problems was in murdering Saul, God's anointed. These men and their violent nature would have brought David down had God not delivered him by providing a peaceful way out: because Saul realised he had fallen into his own trap, and departed peacefully:

> *I will cry unto God most high; unto God that performeth all things for me. He shall send from heaven, and save me from the reproach of him that would swallow me up. Selah. God shall send forth his mercy and his truth. ... They have prepared a net for my steps; my soul is bowed down: they have digged a pit before me, into the midst whereof they are fallen themselves. Selah. (Psa 57:2-3, 6)*

The lesson we could take from this incident is that sometimes in life we have to stand up for our principles in the face of fierce opposition. Some may well try to encourage us to twist the law or do things against God's will — but God will be with us if we resist, and ultimately we will be respected all the more for standing up for our principles.

Food for thought

Verse 3 - The one who would "swallow me up" is Saul.

Verse 4 - Isn't it interesting that whilst David had saved sheep from a lion (1Sam 17:36), he did not react with violence towards his own persecutors.

Psalm 58

The deaf snake

Who is this Psalm about? The word "Altaschith" in the heading of the Psalm appears in Psalms 57, 58 and 59, so it's reasonable to assume that they are meant to be read together. In this case all three would appear to be about Saul, so that's the common thread. Can you think of an incident in David's life, related to Saul, where he didn't want men to listen to lies spoken like a snake charmer?

> *The wicked are estranged from the womb: they go astray as soon as they be born, speaking lies. Their poison is like the poison of a serpent: they are like the deaf adder that stoppeth her ear; Which will not hearken to the voice of charmers, charming never so wisely. (Psa 58:3-5)*

Food for thought

Verse 1-2 - David is criticising a group of individuals who appear to be giving right judgement but in reality are deceitful. This is a great danger that we should avoid. It is so easy to say things to please men but in reality we have another agenda.

Verse 4-5 - In speaking of the "deaf adder" he is speaking of men who will not listen to instruction – an idea that is presented again in Jeremiah 8:17. These people may as well be deaf as they do not listen to instruction. Deafness is a quality that God uses to speak of rebellious Israel elsewhere, for example 2 Kings 17:14.

Psalm 59

They lie in wait for my soul

To the chief Musician, Altaschith, Michtam of David; when Saul sent, and they watched the house to kill him. Deliver me from mine enemies, O my God: defend me from them that rise up against me. (Psa 59:1)

In Psalm 59 David asks God to deliver him from his enemies. Looking at the first verse it is clear that his enemies at this time were Saul and his servants. The men Saul sent to capture David seem to have been particularly formidable:

Deliver me from the workers of iniquity, and save me from bloody men. For, lo, they lie in wait for my soul: the mighty are gathered against me; not for my transgression, nor for my sin, O LORD. (Psa 59:2-3)

God answered this prayer, but it was many years later that Saul finally died and stopped trying to kill David.

Sometimes the answer to our prayers is "yes, but not now."

For the moment, God's answer was to provide the means for him to flee while saving the life of his wife too:

> *Saul also sent messengers unto David's house, to watch him, and to slay him in the morning: and Michal David's wife told him, saying, If thou save not thy life to night, to morrow thou shalt be slain. ... And when the messengers were come in, behold, there was an image in the bed, with a pillow of goats' hair for his bolster. And Saul said unto Michal, Why hast thou deceived me so, and sent away mine enemy, that he is escaped? And Michal answered Saul, He said unto me, Let me go; why should I kill thee? So David fled, and escaped... (1Sa 19:11, 16-18)*

God's answer is not always what we want, but it is what is best for us. Looking into the examples of David's life can help us get the correct perspective:

> *But I will sing of thy power; yea, I will sing aloud of thy mercy in the morning: for thou hast been my defence and refuge in the day of my trouble. (Psa 59:16)*

Food for thought

Verse 6, 14 - When it is realised that this Psalm relates to the events of 1 Samuel 19:11 the use of the word "evening" in v6 and v14 takes on quite a specific significance: this was the time when Saul's servants were around David's house seeking to catch him.

The only other use of "dog" in the Psalms is to be found in Psa 22:20 where David is praying again for deliverance.

Verse 17 - David was delivered in response to prayer. Now he has been delivered he prays to God in thankfulness. How often do we thank God when our prayers have been answered?

Psalm 60

O God, thou hast cast us off

The reading of this Psalm will not benefit us unless we know why God left David. In v1 and v9 we can see that David's army was in a struggle against the armies of Edom and, for once, God didn't grant them victory:

> ...O God, thou hast cast us off, thou hast scattered us, thou hast been displeased; O turn thyself to us again. ... Who will bring me into the strong city? who will lead me into Edom? (Psa 60:1, 9)

Why was God not with David and the army? Is God random in the way He deals with us?

We find the historical context in 2 Samuel 11. In verse 17 the soldiers of the city come out and kill some of David's men. It's one of the only places in the Bible where David's army lost a battle:

> And the men of the city went out, and fought with Joab: and there fell some of the people of the servants of David; and Uriah the Hittite died also. (2Sa 11:17)

Could this be the occasion that stimulated him to write the Psalm? In 2Sam 11:1 we read that it is the city of Rabbah. This doesn't seem to link to the Psalm, because here in v1 it says David strove against Mesopotamia:

> To the Chief Musician. Set to "Lily of the Testimony." A Michtam of David. For teaching. When he fought against Mesopotamia and Syria of Zobah... (Psa 60:1 NKJV)

Bear with me though. The same word occurs in 1Chron 19:6:

> And when the children of Ammon saw that they had made themselves odious to David, Hanun and the children of Ammon sent a thousand talents of silver to hire them chariots and horsemen out of Mesopotamia, and out of Syriamaachah, and out of Zobah. (1Ch 19:6)

This is the same military campaign. Notice Zobah is mentioned both in this verse and in our Psalm. Once David had finished with Ammon, he sent Joab to go and punish the countries that had sent hired soldiers against him. It was during that campaign that God left David's army. Why?

Well, if we backtrack and read the rest of 2 Samuel 11 we see that it was during the time of this campaign that David had commanded Joab to cause Uriah, the husband of Bathsheba, to be killed. It appears that in God's displeasure He left David. It is amazing how, apparently, David had become so used to God's blessing that he thought even this wicked behaviour would pass without consequence. The Psalm is written to show his astonishment at God leaving him.

How about us? Have we become used to God's blessing? Are we so used to God's grace that we sin and presume He will forgive, without thinking of the consequences? David came to regret this whole incident immensely, and later wrote about his attitude:

Keep back thy servant also from presumptuous sins; let them not have dominion over me: then shall I be upright, and I shall be innocent from the great transgression. (Psa 19:13)

Food for thought

Verse 5 - The one who is called "thy beloved" actually is David because that is the meaning of his name.

Verse 8-10 - Reflecting on the expansion of his kingdom, David sees the areas which he will take control of but recognises that the deliverance will be of God.

Psalm 61

How to become a child of God

As we have seen in multiple Psalms, God has been a shelter for David. God has been a strong tower in which to hide from the enemy. David recalls, in this Psalm 61, the episodes in his life where he was utterly overwhelmed:

> *From the end of the earth will I cry unto thee, when my heart is overwhelmed: lead me to the rock that is higher than I. (Psa 61:2)*

These were the times where he despaired of life. He had no way out, no way to save himself, nothing he could do. They were times where he had tried everything, but still his enemies prevailed, looming over him and casting a shadow over his every waking hour.

At these times of utter incapacity, David had turned to God. Through the utter beating down he received in his trials, he had been able to see that there was nowhere else to turn, but to God. In utter desperation, misery, and depression, he had given up his own hold on life, and given it over to his Father. His *Father*, yes, not only his God, because it was through this giving up of his own life, that he gained son-ship.

If you have the chance, read Hebrews 11 and 12 back to back in one go, and see the wonderful progression in Paul's argument. A long list of people, who, having an awful lot going for them, gave it up, instead relinquishing control of their lives to God. Then the exhortation that this is exactly what Christ did too, overcoming by giving up (Heb 12:2), and gaining the sonship because of it:

> *Looking unto Jesus the author and finisher of our faith; who for the joy that was set before him endured the cross, despising the shame, and is set down at the right hand of the throne of God. (Heb 12:2)*

The progression in Hebrews shows that we ourselves, if we give ourselves up to God in subjection to trials and chastening, will gain sonship:

> *If ye endure chastening, God dealeth with you as with sons; for what son is he whom the father chasteneth not? ... Furthermore we have had fathers of our flesh which corrected us, and we gave them reverence: shall we not much rather be in subjection unto the Father of spirits, and live? (Heb 12:7, 9)*

This son-ship brings with it a spiritual abode in the heavens along with Christ:

> *But ye are come unto mount Sion, and unto the city of the living God, the heavenly Jerusalem, and to an innumerable company of angels, To the general assembly and church of the firstborn, which are written in heaven, and to God the Judge of all, and to the spirits of just men made perfect. (Heb 12:22-23)*

It is this sonship, and the heavenly abode which goes with it, that David gained through his trials. Whenever he gave up to God, trusting in Him alone, he was dwelling in heavenly places. God was his shelter. God was his tower. God kept him warm and dry under the shelter of His wings. God had given him the heritage of a son:

> *For thou hast been a shelter for me, and a strong tower from the enemy. I will abide in thy tabernacle for ever: I will trust in the covert of thy wings. Selah. For thou, O God, hast heard my vows: thou hast given me the heritage of those that fear thy name. (Psa 61:3-5)*

David would dwell with God in this life, and then forever, *because* he had given up and subjected himself to God:

> *He shall **abide before God for ever**: O prepare mercy and truth, which may preserve him. (Psa 61:7)*

Food for thought

Verse 1, 3 - David feels able to cry to God for help (v1) because he knows that God has heard him in the past (v3). An example for us to follow. We must be aware of the ways in which God has been with us in the past else we will have no basis for confidence that He will help us in our present distresses.

Verse 6 - David recognised, when God made promises to him -2Sam 7:19 that the promise was a long term promise. This is echoed here in the Psalm.

Psalm 62

David's parable of the rock

Have you noticed how many times in this Psalm David calls God his rock? In comparison, he says the wicked are like a bowing wall:

> *How long will ye imagine mischief against a man? ye shall be slain all of you: as a bowing wall shall ye be, and as a tottering fence.* (Psa 62:3)

A bowing wall or a tottering fence is an unsteady thing to lean against. It's likely to give way and take you with it. But David is saying that what he leans on is the bedrock which cannot move.

> *He only is my rock and my salvation: he is my defence;* **I shall not be moved**. (Psa 62:6)

Is this Psalm where Jesus got his parable of the wise man who built his house on a rock and the foolish man who built it on sand? (See Matt 7:24-29.)

Food for thought

Verse 2 - The word "only" catches the command of God "thou shalt worship no other god" – Exodus 34:14. Can we be as definite as David was? Or are there other things in our lives which at times take precedence over God?

Verse 12 - It is interesting to note that God is merciful because He renders according to works. God's judgement is not with respect of persons. He judges righteously.

Psalm 63

Worshippers of things

David appears to have been in the tabernacle and seen some of the articles that displayed the splendour of God:

> *To see thy power and thy glory, so as I have seen thee in the **sanctuary**. (Psa 63:2)*

Here the word for "sanctuary" is the same as the "holy place" in Exodus 26:33 and 28:43:

> *And thou shalt hang up the vail under the taches, that thou mayest bring in thither within the vail the ark of the testimony: and the vail shall divide unto you between the **holy place** and the most holy. (Exo 26:33)*

> *And they shall be upon Aaron, and upon his sons, when they come in unto the tabernacle of the congregation, or when they come near unto the altar to minister in the **holy place**; that they bear not iniquity, and die: it shall be a statute for ever unto him and his seed after him. (Exo 28:43)*

Yet, though he was overawed by it, he knew the splendour of these 'things' was only a shadow of the true splendour of God. And so in v1-2 he declares that even though he had seen the sanctuary, his thirst and need for God was completely unsatisfied:

> A Psalm of David, when he was in the wilderness of Judah.
> *O God, thou art my God; early will I seek thee: my soul thirsteth for thee, my flesh longeth for thee in a dry and thirsty land, where no water is; To see thy power and thy glory, so as I have seen thee in the sanctuary. (Psa 63:1-2)*

This is the stage that all worshippers of 'things' must come to. No matter how splendid the buildings we worship in, the robes we wear, how eloquent our services, or how beautiful our songs, these are all shadows and not the real thing. The real thing, the real beauty, described in v6-11, is that we can come and approach God in prayer, no matter where we are, and ask for what we desire:

> *When I remember thee upon my bed, and meditate on thee in the night watches. Because thou hast been my help, therefore in the shadow of thy wings will I rejoice. My soul followeth hard after thee: thy right hand upholdeth me. (Psa 63:6-8)*

This true splendour of God was demonstrated in David's life in the way he put his trust in God and was delivered from all his troubles. He describes this as the true "taking refuge under the shadow of your wings" (v7), a reference to the wings overshadowing the mercy seat on the ark of the covenant (Exo 25:20, 2Sam 7:18).

A dry and thirsty land

It is easy to assume from the title to the Psalm that this was written about David's time spent escaping Saul in the wilderness of Judah. But it fits better with a later occasion. In 2Sam 15:23 we read that David, now king, and all his household, escaped into the wilderness from Absalom:

> *And all the country wept with a loud voice, and all the people passed over: the king also himself passed over the brook Kidron, and all the people passed over, toward the way of the wilderness. (2Sa 15:23)*

This fits better with Psalm 63:11 where David refers to himself as the king:

> *But the king shall rejoice in God; every one that sweareth by him shall glory: but the mouth of them that speak lies shall be stopped. (Psa 63:11)*

Also notice verse 1:

> *...my soul thirsteth for thee, my flesh longeth for thee in **a dry and thirsty land, where no water is**. (Psa 63:1)*

It shows the peril David and his wives, elderly and young ones were in, linking with the account in 2Sam 16:2:

> *And the king said unto Ziba, What meanest thou by these? And Ziba said, The asses be for the king's household to ride on; and the bread and summer fruit for the young men to eat; and*

*the wine, that **such as be faint in the wilderness may drink**. (2Sa 16:2)*

And:

And honey, and butter, and sheep, and cheese of kine, for David, and for the people that were with him, to eat: for they said, The people is hungry, and weary, and thirsty, in the wilderness. (2Sa 17:29)

Can you imagine his distress at seeing his loved ones going without food and water, and then their relief at the salvation of God, who prepared for them a banquet in the wilderness? (See 2Sam 17:27-29, Psa 23:4-6.)

Food for thought

Verse 2 - So when David speaks of having seen God in the sanctuary he is commenting upon the time when he went and "sat before the Lord" (2 Samuel 7:18).

Verse 3 - God's "lovingkindness" was shown to David in the promise of the son in 2Sam 7. So, even when fleeing from Absalom, David's focus is on the promises that God made to him.

Psalm 64

Words that pierce like arrows

In this Psalm David is afraid of the words of the wicked. Look how he likens their words as weapons:

> *Who whet their tongue like a sword, and bend their bows*
> *to shoot their arrows, even bitter words. (Psa 64:3)*

Can words really be that damaging? Certainly in David's case, Absalom's words were what almost cost him his life. Absalom secretly set about to undermine David's credibility and to damage his popularity by digging up all the dirt:

> *They search out iniquities; they accomplish a diligent search:*
> *both the inward thought of every one of them, and the heart, is*
> *deep. (Psa 64:6)*

This sustained effort worked. Absalom gathered a group of co-conspirators (v5 "they commune") and suddenly, in one day, he fired his arrows at David in an incredibly bold plot to take over the throne:

> *That they may shoot in secret at the perfect:* **suddenly do they shoot at him***, and fear not.* **They encourage themselves** *in an evil matter:***they commune** *of laying snares privily; they say, Who shall see them? (Psa 64:4-5)*

The whole story is in 2 Samuel 15 -17. The Psalm doesn't end there, however. It goes on to say that, by the same weapon of words, God would protect David and cause their plot to fail.

> *But God shall shoot at them with an arrow; suddenly shall they be wounded. So they shall make their own tongue to fall upon themselves: all that see them shall flee away. (Psa 64:7-8)*

To find out how God did it, take note of Ahithophel's words and Hushai's words in the Samuel account.

Food for thought

Verse 6 - Whilst "love covers a multitude of sins" (James 5:20, 1Pet 4:8), the wicked are searching for things to cast against the righteous. Herein is a warning for us. It is so easy to look for faults in others rather than look for the best.

Verse 2 - In asking to be hidden in the time of trouble, maybe David is reflecting on the way that God 'took' Enoch, possibly away from the persecution of Lamech – Gen 5:24.

Psalm 65

A prophecy of the chosen one

Blessed is the man whom thou choosest, and causest to approach unto thee, that he may dwell in thy courts: we shall be satisfied with the goodness of thy house, even of thy holy temple. (Psa 65:4)

The chosen one was Jesus, and this Psalm is a prophecy about him. I wonder if Jesus' calming of the storm in (Matt 14:24-32) is a fulfilment of verse 7?

Which stilleth the noise of the seas, the noise of their waves, and the tumult of the people. (Psa 65:7)

If it is, then Jesus was drawing his disciples' attention to this Psalm and plainly declaring 'I am the chosen one' to his disciples. This fits in with the context because Jesus' feeding of the 5000 in the wilderness in the previous verses of Matthew 14, would relate to v11-13:

*Thou crownest the year with thy goodness; and thy paths drop fatness. They drop upon **the pastures of the wilderness**: and* *the little hills rejoice on every side. The pastures are clothed with flocks; the valleys also are covered over with corn; they shout for joy, they also sing. (Psa 65:11-13)*

This is a good explanation of why the disciples, who had witnessed the Psalm being fulfilled, were immediately compelled to say:

...Of a truth thou art the Son of God. (Mat 14:33)

Food for thought

Verse 4 - The "blessed man" is a recurring theme in the Psalms. There is value in looking at all the things that are said about the blessed man (see Psalm 1:1, 32:1, 34:8, 94:12, 112:1).

Verse 5 - We might think that this verse is speaking only of the future salvation of mankind. However verse 9-13 shows that God's salvation extends, here and now, to the harvest that we take so much for granted year in year out.

Psalm 66

I will pay my vows

I will go into thy house with burnt offerings: I will pay thee my vows. (Psa 66:13)

David's undertaking to "pay" his vows occurs in many other of David's Psalms. David appears to have promised (vowed) to praise God in the assembly of Israel:

I will declare thy name unto my brethren: in the midst of the congregation will I praise thee. Ye that fear the LORD, praise him; all ye the seed of Jacob, glorify him; and fear him, all ye the seed of Israel. For he hath not despised nor abhorred the affliction of the afflicted; neither hath he hid his face from him; but when he cried unto him, he heard. My praise shall be of thee in the great congregation: I will pay my vows before them that fear him. (Psa 22:22-25)

He seems to have vowed this in return for help in his hour of danger, as explained later in that same Psalm:

> *But be not thou far from me, O LORD: O my strength, haste thee to help me. Deliver my soul from the sword; my darling from the power of the dog. Save me from the lion's mouth: for thou hast heard me from the horns of the unicorns. (Psa 22:19-21)*

The need to pay this vow was with him constantly, and writing the Psalms was one way of keeping it. This Psalm 66 is one example, which starts by praising God, and finishes by declaring openly David's own need for God, and a call to others to hear David's story of personal deliverance:

> *Come and hear, all ye that fear God, and **I will declare what he hath done for my soul**. I cried unto him with my mouth, and he was extolled with my tongue. If I regard iniquity in my heart, the Lord will not hear me: But verily God hath heard me; he hath attended to the voice of my prayer. Blessed be God, which hath not turned away my prayer, nor his mercy from me. (Psa 66:16-20)*

Do we declare it aloud when we are personally helped by God?

Food for thought

Verse 5 - The request "come and see" what God has done is the most powerful evidence to the existence of God and that He is working in the world. So when two of Jesus' disciples asked where he was staying, he said "come and see" (John 1:39), which appears to have been the invitation to become involved in the work by seeing the life the man Jesus was living.

Verse 12 - The way in which the Psalmist talks about going through fire and water is echoed by Isaiah (43:2). Both these passages must have been a comfort to those cast into the fiery furnace (Daniel 3:20) and can be a comfort to us when we're in difficulty.

Psalm 67

Who else served Israel's God?

> To the chief Musician on Neginoth, A Psalm or Song. *God be merciful unto us, and bless us; and cause his face to shine upon us; Selah. That thy way may be known upon earth, thy saving health among all nations. (Psa 67:1-2)*

The Psalmist wants God to bless Israel, so that by seeing the health and prosperity of the people, other nations will invite his God to be their God too. Did this ever happen? If ever there was a time when God's face shone upon His people Israel it was the time when Solomon reigned. At this time it says:

> *And all the kings of the earth sought the presence of Solomon, to hear his wisdom, that God had put in his heart. (2Ch 9:23)*

Does that mean that perhaps Solomon passed on the knowledge of God too? When the Queen of Sheba visited this is what she said:

> *Blessed be the LORD thy God, which delighted in thee to set thee on his throne, to be king for the LORD thy God: because*

thy God loved Israel, to establish them for ever, therefore made he thee king over them, to do judgment and justice. (2Ch 9:8)

She certainly believed in Solomon's God. So it appears that the Queen of Sheba, at the very least, fulfilled this Psalm, seeing the blessing of God and perhaps taking it back with her to her own people (v3-4).

How many other visitors could there have been who did the same?

Food for thought

Verse 1-2 - God's glory – His shining face – is seen in those that believe in Him. It should be seen by others; hence the gospel should change the way in which we live.

Verse 4 - In seeking for the nations to be glad we see a picture of the kingdom, when Christ will rule over all nations.

Psalm 68

God's glory shown in might and gentleness

This Psalm seems to be focusing on how God's reputation spread to the nations roundabout Israel as a result of Israel's journey from Egypt and subsequent possession of Canaan. It's interesting to see the different sides to God's glory, both in the might of war, and the gentleness of His care:

> *A father of the fatherless, and a judge of the widows, is God in his holy habitation. ...*
> *The chariots of God are twenty thousand, even thousands of angels: the Lord is among them, as in Sinai, in the holy place.* (Psa 68:5, 17)

Also, notice the two mountains mentioned as God's dwelling place; Sinai and Zion (Jerusalem) corresponding to these same two aspects of His glory:

> *For ye are not come unto the mount that might be touched, and that burned with fire, nor unto blackness, and darkness, and tempest, ...*

> *But ye are come unto mount Sion, and unto the city of the living God, the heavenly Jerusalem, and to an innumerable company of angels, To the general assembly and church of the firstborn, which are written in heaven, and to God the Judge of all, and to the spirits of just men made perfect. (Heb 12:18, 22-23)*

What did Israel drink in the wilderness journey?

We tend to think, reading the Exodus account, that the children of Israel were feeling thirsty a lot of the time. But notice this detail in the Psalm:

> *O God, when thou wentest forth before thy people, when thou didst march through the wilderness; Selah: The earth shook, the heavens also dropped at the presence of God: even Sinai itself was moved at the presence of God, the God of Israel. Thou, O God, didst send a plentiful rain, whereby thou didst confirm thine inheritance, when it was weary. (Psa 68:7-9)*

God sent rain on the children of Israel in the wilderness, and this is not recorded anywhere in the Exodus account. So, once again the Psalms give extra detail to fill the picture out.

How does your view of the Exodus journey change, knowing what you do now?

Food for thought

Verse 6 - We need to realise that before accepting Christ we are "solitary" no matter how many friends and family members we have. In Christ those who once were God's enemies – Rom 5:10– are now

His children, His sons and daughters – 1John 3:1.

Verse 21 - In saying that God will wound the heads of His enemies we are being reminded of the promise in Genesis 3:15. Jael enacted this out also - Judges 5:26.

Psalm 69

A pattern for prayer in distress

Before reading this Psalm, I suggest reading the events of David's life in 2 Samuel 12-15. When you then read the Psalm, you will see many references back to those events.

Reading the Psalms like this makes the stories of David spring to life, showing us the thoughts and prayers of that God-fearing man.

This Psalm contains perhaps the most emotive and deep thoughts that David uttered, and he is perhaps at his lowest point of despair:

> *Let not the waterflood overflow me, neither let the deep swallow me up, and let not the pit shut her mouth upon me. ... Reproach hath broken my heart; and I am full of heaviness: and I looked for some to take pity, but there was none; and for comforters, but I found none. (Psa 69:15, 20)*

We can then also read on in 2 Samuel to see whether David's fervent prayer in this Psalm was answered.

Then notice how the Psalm, as well as referring to actual events in the life of David, is a prophecy of the trouble Jesus would suffer:

They gave me also gall for my meat; and in my thirst they gave me vinegar to drink. (Psa 69:21)

Which is quoted in the Matthew account of Jesus' crucifixion:

They gave him vinegar to drink mingled with gall: and when he had tasted thereof, he would not drink. (Mat 27:34)

So, we could now also read ahead to Matthew 27 and look at the trial of Jesus with David's thoughts and experiences in mind.

The final stop in the journey is when we ourselves encounter troubles that remind us of any of these thoughts. We can then pray those same words that David and Jesus prayed, and if the LORD wills, we will be delivered in similar fashion.

2 Samuel 12-15 > Psalm 69 > Matthew 26-27 > prayer in your life.

Food for thought

Verse 1 - "the waters are come in unto my soul" is echoed by Jonah – Jonah 2:3 – one of many references to the Psalms found in Jonah's prayer highlighting that, in distress, he turned to the Psalms for comfort.

Verse 12 - There is awful poignancy in David saying "they that sat in the gate speak against me" as that is where Absalom set himself – 2Sam 15:2 - to turn the hearts of the nation against his father David. So we see that not only did he speak with those that came to the king for judgement but also to the others who sat in the gate – probably men appointed to the job by David.

Verse 20 - In looking for comforters and finding none David foreshadows Jesus in the garden of Gethsemane - Matthew 26:40.

Psalm 70

Learn of me, for I am meek

In verse 5 David says:

> But I am poor and needy: make haste unto me, O God: thou art my help and my deliverer; O LORD, make no tarrying. (Psa 70:5)

Notice the humility here of a man who ordinarily you wouldn't expect to show it. He had after all been anointed the King of God's people. Yet God rewards humility. Jesus demonstrated this when he said:

> Blessed are the poor in spirit: for theirs is the kingdom of heaven. Blessed are they that mourn: for they shall be comforted. **Blessed are the meek:** for they shall inherit the earth. (Mat 5:3-5)

The importance of this principle is confirmed in the book of Micah, where it is listed as one of three requirements in order to come to God:

*He hath shewed thee, O man, what is good; and what doth the LORD require of thee, but to do justly, and to love mercy, and **to walk humbly with thy God**? (Mic 6:8)*

Humility is, however, very difficult to achieve. We naturally want the opposite - to build ourselves up in the sight of others. How, then, do we achieve meekness when it is contrary to our nature?

Moses was described as the perfect example of meekness:

Now the man Moses was very meek, above all the men which were upon the face of the earth. (Num 12:3)

He was a man born in a royal household, yet followed this with forty years following sheep. David also was a shepherd. And Jesus himself, who was so meek that he was led like a lamb to the slaughter, and who is described as our shepherd, told us to learn meekness of him:

*Come unto me, all ye that labour and are heavy laden, and I will give you rest. Take my yoke upon you, and **learn of me; for I am meek and lowly in heart**: and ye shall find rest unto your souls. (Mat 11:28-29)*

So the offer of inheriting the earth is given to the meek, and in turn, the offer of learning to be meek is given to us by Jesus. Let us take him up on his offer - to learn humility from him, and David and Moses too. It may not be easy, but it will be worth it.

Food for thought

Verse 2, 4 - Notice the contrast. David speaks of those that "seek" his life and those that "seek" God.

Verse 5 - This Psalm is an extract of the words of Psalm 40:13-17 and, as such, shows how the servant who wants to serve his master because he loves him recognises that he has no rights of his own.

Psalm 71

Showing God to the next generation

David was grey haired and ready to retire from being King. However, his chosen heir, Solomon, was still too young to succeed him. This period of waiting for him to grow up was a difficult time for David and his wife Bathsheba, especially since there were many older sons of David who wanted the throne. This is the context of verse 18:

> Now also when I am old and grayheaded, O God, forsake me not; until I have shewed thy strength unto this generation, and thy power to every one that is to come. (Psa 71:18)

David wanted Solomon to have the same faith in God he had himself, and was asking God to give him time to finish the task of teaching him. The next Psalm confirms that the context is of the heir, Solomon:

> A Psalm for Solomon. Give the king thy judgments, O God, and thy righteousness unto the king's son. (Psa 72:1)

I personally think that we can find much of the advice David gave to him during that crucial time in the book of Proverbs.

Food for thought

Verse 16 - The society in which we live teaches us to have confidence in ourselves, to make the most of opportunities that arise, and to seize the moment. However all of those ideas are at variance with the teaching of God. We are to humble ourselves – James 4:10, 1Pet 5:6 – and go "in the strength of the Lord."

Verse 20 - The Psalmist recognises that he will attain to everlasting life through tribulation. He recognises the chastening hand of God in his life, and that it is for his ultimate good.

Psalm 72

Prophecies of Solomon's reign

This is one of the last Psalms of David, as you can see in the last verse:

> The prayers of David the son of Jesse are ended. (Psa 72:20)

We can also see that this Psalm is about Solomon, because of the title:

> A Psalm for Solomon. *Give the king thy judgments, O God, and thy righteousness unto the king's son.* (Psa 72:1)

There are details in here, like the Queen of Sheba in v10, which seem to have been a prophecy by David of how his son would become a renowned King among the nations:

> *The kings of Tarshish and of the isles shall bring presents: the kings of Sheba and Seba shall offer gifts.* (Psa 72:10)

This was precisely fulfilled in Solomon's day:

> *And she gave the king an hundred and twenty talents of gold, and of spices very great store, and precious stones: there came no more such abundance of spices as these which the queen of Sheba gave to king Solomon. (1Ki 10:10)*

Can you imagine Solomon, as a young man, hearing his father David speaking or singing this prayer, and feeling the weight of expectation on his shoulders?

Question: Which details of this Psalm did Solomon fulfil, and which did he leave undone? The list of things he left undone have yet to be fulfilled with Jesus, the ultimate "son of David".

Food for thought

Verse 2 - The sentiments of judging the world in righteousness are echoed in Isaiah 11:4-5. Very interesting when we realise that this Psalm has the kingship of Solomon as its basis, looking forward to Messiah – Jesus Christ.

Verse 8 - The promise of world-wide dominion is quoted by Zechariah (9:10) in the context of a prophecy about Jesus as king.

III

Psalms 73-89

Psalm 73

Drawing near to God

The author of the Psalm, Asaph, had trouble coming to terms with why it should be that bad people seem to prosper:

> For I was envious at the foolish, when I saw the prosperity of the wicked. ... They are not in trouble as other men; neither are they plagued like other men. ... Their eyes stand out with fatness: they have more than heart could wish. (Psa 73:3, 5, 7)

When he went into the sanctuary he understood the answer to his problem:

> When I thought to know this, it was too painful for me; Until I went into the sanctuary of God; then understood I their end. (Psa 73:16-17)

The "sanctuary of God" is the name given to the temple, or the tabernacle before it.

> *And the Kohathites set forward, bearing the **sanctuary**: and the other did set up the tabernacle against they came. (Num 10:21)*
>
> *David also commanded all the princes of Israel to help Solomon his son, saying, ... arise therefore, and build ye the **sanctuary** of the LORD God, to bring the ark of the covenant of the LORD, and the holy vessels of God, into the house that is to be built to the name of the LORD. (1Ch 22:17, 19)*

But what was it about the temple that caught Asaph's mind?

As he walked into the courtyard, he would be confronted by a large altar and large golden basin of water next to it. If he wanted to walk any further towards the sanctuary to be near to God, he would have to make sacrifices, and to be clean. These strikingly visual obstacles between him and God may have been the thing that caught his imagination, because in his conclusion (v27-28) he compares those who draw near to God (i.e. are clean of heart, v13), to those who stand far off (not prepared to sacrifice to be clean).

> *For, lo, **they that are far from thee shall perish**: thou hast destroyed all them that go a whoring from thee. But it is **good for me to draw near to God**: I have put my trust in the Lord GOD, that I may declare all thy works. (Psa 73:27-28)*

Asaph may have realised that to be near to God required a certain amount of suffering (the altar) and cleansing (the basin) in order to be acceptable to Him. This had been his experience in v13-14:

> *Verily I have cleansed my heart in vain, and washed my hands in innocency. For all the day long have I been plagued, and chastened every morning. (Psa 73:13-14)*

Was he now suddenly able to see that it was not a vain cause? His difficulties in life had actually preparing him to reach God:

> *Nevertheless **I am continually with thee**: thou hast holden me by my right hand. Thou shalt guide me with thy counsel, and afterward receive me to glory. (Psa 73:23-24)*

Food for thought

Verses 1-7 - The way that the faithful Psalmist was almost drawn away by reflecting on the prosperity of others should warn us against lusting after those things which our neighbours have.

Verse 9 - The epitomy of the wicked is the beast (Revelation 13) who also has a "mouth speaking great things." So we see that the individual wicked are likened to that great system which opposes Christ.

Psalm 74

When God is against us

Sometimes we think that God is for us, when in reality He's not. Sometimes we think that, because He answered our prayers in some mighty way, He is with us. We think we're special. We can start to think that nothing we do will go without His blessing.

This was the problem that Israel struggled with ever after their miraculous deliverance from Egypt. Throughout the wilderness journey they continually quoted the fact that they were now God's people, in order to justify the way they were behaving:

> *And they said, Hath the LORD indeed spoken only by Moses? hath he not spoken also by us? And the LORD heard it. (Num 12:2)*
>
> *And they gathered themselves together against Moses and against Aaron, and said unto them, Ye take too much upon you, seeing all the congregation are holy, every one of them, and the LORD is among them: wherefore then lift ye up yourselves above the congregation of the LORD? (Num 16:3)*

This continued right through till the time of Jesus and beyond:

> *And think not to say within yourselves, We have Abraham to our father: for I say unto you, that God is able of these stones to raise up children unto Abraham. (Mat 3:9)*

But it's probably the same with us. 'Why', we ask ourselves, 'if God is with us, is everything going wrong?' And this is the subject of this Psalm:

> Maschil of Asaph. *O God, why hast thou cast us off for ever?* **why doth thine anger smoke against the sheep of thy pasture?** ... *Why withdrawest thou thy hand, even thy right hand? pluck it out of thy bosom. (Psa 74:1, 11)*

At times, before we know it, we have strayed so far from the paths of God, that God has had to turn His hand *against* us, to chasten us in order to turn us around and bring us back. It can be the very blessings of God that have directly contributed to our going astray. It can be the visible hand of God in our lives, through miraculous answered prayer, that lifts us up in pride, and makes us forget that it is God doing the delivering, and not us. We can get too big for our boots.

> *O deliver not the soul of thy* **turtledove** *unto the multitude of the wicked: forget not the congregation of thy poor for ever. (Psa 74:19)*

In v19, Asaph calls God's people His Turtledove. Jeremiah tells us that this is only if we act like the animal itself. If we are to claim to be God's people, and have the benefits of His blessings, we should be acting like people of God:

*Yea, the stork in the heaven knoweth her appointed times; and the **turtle**and the crane and the swallow observe the time of their coming; **but my people know not the judgment of the LORD**. (Jer 8:7)*

Food for thought

Verses 1-2 - On seeing that nation suffer God's anger, the Psalmist calls upon God to remember the people that He had purchased. This is similar to Moses, when God would have destroyed them, asking God to remember what He had promised to the fathers. See Exodus 32:10-13.

Verses 18-23 - Don't forget that when people criticise, or even persecute you for telling (or living) the truth, they are really criticising God first and foremost.

Psalm 75

The cup of dregs

In v8 we're told that God will pour out a cup of dregs:

> *For in the hand of the LORD there is a cup, and the wine is red; it is full of mixture; and he poureth out of the same: but the dregs thereof, all the wicked of the earth shall wring them out, and drink them. (Psalm 75:8)*

This symbolism of a cup of dregs is recorded in Isaiah 51:17, speaking of God's judgments on Jerusalem:

> *Awake, awake, stand up, O Jerusalem, which hast drunk at the hand of the LORD the cup of his fury; thou hast drunken the dregs of the cup of trembling, and wrung them out. (Isaiah 51:17)*

And also in Isaiah 51:22-23, where it speaks of God's judgment on those that afflict His people:

> *Thus saith thy Lord the LORD, and thy God that pleadeth the*

cause of his people, Behold, I have taken out of thine hand the cup of trembling, even the dregs of the cup of my fury; thou shalt no more drink it again: But I will put it into the hand of them that afflict thee; which have said to thy soul, Bow down, that we may go over: and thou hast laid thy body as the ground, and as the street, to them that went over. (Isaiah 51:22-23)

Which of these two cups do you think this Psalm is talking about?

Food for thought

Verse 6 - Respect of persons often has as its motivation self advancement. Here the Psalmist shows that it is God who blesses. We must be careful to think about how we respond to others and to appreciate that God is in control in our lives.

Verse 7 - In telling us that God "putteth down one and setteth up another" the Psalmist is stating what God himself says (Daniel 2:21).

Psalm 76

Instilling fear in the nations

Psalm 76 is about God's deliverance of Israel from Egypt by destroying Pharaoh's army. How many references to Exodus can you find?

In Exodus chapter 15 we read the account of this destruction. Notice what Moses says about it:

> Who is like unto thee, O LORD, among the gods? who is like thee, glorious in holiness, fearful in praises, doing wonders? Thou stretchedst out thy right hand, the earth swallowed them. Thou in thy mercy hast led forth the people which thou hast redeemed: thou hast guided them in thy strength unto thy holy habitation. **The people shall hear, and be afraid: sorrow shall take hold on the inhabitants of Palestina. Then the dukes of Edom shall be amazed; the mighty men of Moab, trembling shall take hold upon them; all the inhabitants of Canaan shall melt away. Fear and dread shall fall upon them;** by the greatness of thine arm they shall be as still as a stone; till thy people pass over, O LORD, till the people pass over, which thou hast purchased. (Exo 15:11-16)

Moses tells us that the reason God made such a spectacle of destroying Egypt's army, is that it paved the way for their safe entry into the land of promise. The other nations would be so scared of the God they had heard about, that they would be unable to fight His people.

The Psalmist, in retrospect, confirms that this was in fact what happened:

> *Thou, even thou, art to be feared: and who may stand in thy sight when once thou art angry? Thou didst cause judgment to be heard from heaven;* **the earth feared, and was still**, *... Vow, and pay unto the LORD your God: let all that be round about him bring presents unto* **him that ought to be feared**. *He shall cut off the spirit of princes: he is terrible to the kings of the earth. (Psa 76:7-8, 11-12)*

Food for thought

Verse 1 - We are so used to talking of Judah (the two tribes) and Israel (the ten tribes) that we pass over this distinction in the Psalm without thinking that the Psalm was written before the division! But actually the split was already appearing before David was on the throne in Jerusalem. (1 Samuel 11:8, 17:52, 18:16)

Verse 11 - "Vow and pay" – how easy it is to make promises and then not keep them. Solomon has instructive words to say on this point in Ecclesiastes 5:2-4.

Psalm 77

The chief musician

Remember to always read the inspired title to each Psalm.

To the chief Musician, to Jeduthun, A Psalm of Asaph. *I cried unto God with my voice, even unto God with my voice; and he gave ear unto me. (Psa 77:1)*

In this title we learn that the writer is Asaph, and that Jeduthan could be the "chief musician" referred to in so many Psalms. These two men and their families were in the service of King David (1Chron 25:1-3, Neh 11:17):

> *Moreover David and the captains of the host separated to the service of the sons of Asaph, and of Heman, and of Jeduthun, who should prophesy with harps, with psalteries, and with cymbals: and the number of the workmen according to their service was: Of the sons of Asaph; Zaccur, and Joseph, and Nethaniah, and Asarelah, the sons of Asaph under the hands of Asaph, which prophesied according to the order of the king. Of Jeduthun: the sons of Jeduthun; Gedaliah, and Zeri, and Jeshaiah, Hashabiah,*

> and Mattithiah, six, under the hands of their father Jeduthun, who prophesied with a harp, to give thanks and to praise the LORD. (1Ch 25:1-3)

These continued in that service right through to Nehemiah's time:

> And Mattaniah the son of Micha, the son of Zabdi, the son of **Asaph**, was the principal to begin the thanksgiving in prayer: and Bakbukiah the second among his brethren, and Abda the son of Shammua, the son of Galal, the son of **Jeduthun**. (Neh 11:17)

So why would this Asaph (or one of his descendants) be so troubled? There may be a clue in the Psalm:

> Will the Lord cast off for ever? and will he be favourable no more? Is his mercy clean gone for ever? doth his promise fail for evermore? (Psa 77:7-8)

Was he perhaps writing at the time when Israel was going into captivity to Babylon?

Food for thought

Verse 18 - The Psalmist is describing what happened when the law was given at Sinai.

Verse 15 - God redeemed Israel when He brought them out of Egypt. He repeatedly reminds Israel of this – for the simple reason that they easily forgot what He had done for them. The deliverance from Egypt is typical of our deliverance from the power of sin. Do we need to be reminded of that wonderful work, or do we never forget it?

Psalm 78

If God has helped you before, why wouldn't He help again?

The whole trouble with Israel in the wilderness, and afterwards, can be summed up by this verse:

> *Because they believed not in God, and trusted not in his salvation. (Psa 78:22)*

They are presented to us as the ultimate example as a people for whom God did everything, and gave everything, so that there was every reason for them to trust in Him — yet, quite amazingly, they still didn't believe Him when He said He would look after them:

> *Yea, they spake against God; they said, Can God furnish a table in the wilderness? (Psa 78:19)*

This was even though He had showed awesome signs in Egypt and delivered them from slavery by mighty plagues:

> *They remembered not his hand, nor the day when he delivered them from the enemy. How he had wrought his signs in Egypt, and his wonders in the field of Zoan. (Psa 78:42-43)*

How could a people who had seen all these miracles limit God? Would they not, above all people, magnify God's power and willingness to save?

In the end Jesus showed them that even Gentiles, who had none of the heritage and privilege of Israel, could get this right:

> *The centurion answered and said, Lord, I am not worthy that thou shouldest come under my roof: but speak the word only, and my servant shall be healed. For I am a man under authority, having soldiers under me: and I say to this man, Go, and he goeth; and to another, Come, and he cometh; and to my servant, Do this, and he doeth it. When Jesus heard it, he marvelled, and said to them that followed, Verily I say unto you,* **I have not found so great faith, no, not in Israel.** *And I say unto you, That many shall come from the east and west, and shall sit down with Abraham, and Isaac, and Jacob, in the kingdom of heaven. But the children of the kingdom shall be cast out into outer darkness: there shall be weeping and gnashing of teeth. And Jesus said unto the centurion, Go thy way; and as thou hast believed, so be it done unto thee. And his servant was healed in the selfsame hour. (Mat 8:8-13)*

Do we limit God?

Do we limit God like Israel did? How about when we're about to pray about something then decide not to because 'it's too silly' or 'it's too insignificant'? Are we saying God (who created our ability to laugh, love and feel sad) is too busy or too uncaring to care about us? How many times does God have to prove that He does care and He does want to help and that He can help?

It's abundantly clear from the Psalm that Israel was expected to remember their deliverance from Egypt and the miraculous sea crossing as proof that they could trust God in any and every situation. It is hard to transfer prior learning to future events, but this is essentially what faith is and we must develop it to be pleasing to God. Faith in the little things of life is still faith, and "faith is counted for righteousness".

> *And he believed in the LORD; and he counted it to him for righteousness. (Gen 15:6)*
>
> *But to him that worketh not, but believeth on him that justifieth the ungodly, his faith is counted for righteousness. (Rom 4:5)*

Food for thought

Verse 19 - In complaining about the lack of food in the wilderness Israel were doubting God's ability to feed them. David (Psalm 23:5) knew that God could feed him in the wilderness, and He actually did (2 Samuel 17:27-29).

Verse 8,18,37 - We see the seat of Israel's problem. Their heart was not right with God. This contrasts with the way in which God dealt with them – "in the integrity of His heart" - verse 72.

Psalm 79

The destruction of Jerusalem

A Psalm of Asaph. *O God, the heathen are come into thine inheritance; thy holy temple have they defiled;* **they have laid Jerusalem on heaps.** *(Psa 79:1)*

Micah prophesied about this event, which is also recorded in Jeremiah:

> *Micah the Morasthite prophesied in the days of Hezekiah king of Judah, and spake to all the people of Judah, saying, Thus saith the LORD of hosts; Zion shall be plowed like a field, and* ***Jerusalem shall become heaps****, and the mountain of the house as the high places of a forest. (Jer 26:18)*

> *Therefore shall Zion for your sake be plowed as a field, and* ***Jerusalem shall become heaps****, and the mountain of the house as the high places of the forest. (Mic 3:12)*

This event is recorded at the end of Chronicles, when God brought judgement upon Jerusalem for their continual abominations:

> *Moreover all the chief of the priests, and the people, transgressed very much after all the abominations of the heathen; and polluted the house of the LORD which he had hallowed in Jerusalem. And the LORD God of their fathers sent to them by his messengers, rising up betimes, and sending; because he had compassion on his people, and on his dwelling place: But they mocked the messengers of God, and despised his words, and misused his prophets, until the wrath of the LORD arose against his people, till there was no remedy. Therefore he brought upon them the king of the Chaldees... And they burnt the house of God, and brake down the wall of Jerusalem, and burnt all the palaces thereof with fire, and destroyed all the goodly vessels thereof. (2Ch 36:14-19)*

Food for thought

Verse 3 - That there would be no one to bury Israel's slain actually happened in the Chaldean captivity (see Jer 14:16).

Verse 8 - In saying that they were "brought very low" The Psalmist is seeing the fulfilment of the curses of Deuteronomy 28 in their experiences (See Deut 28:43).

Psalm 80

The vineyard

Notice the picture of the vine and vineyard mentioned in verses 8-16:

> Thou hast brought a vine out of Egypt: thou hast cast out the heathen, and planted it. Thou preparedst room before it, and didst cause it to take deep root, and it filled the land. The hills were covered with the shadow of it, and the boughs thereof were like the goodly cedars. She sent out her boughs unto the sea, and her branches unto the river. Why hast thou then broken down her hedges, so that all they which pass by the way do pluck her? The boar out of the wood doth waste it, and the wild beast of the field doth devour it. Return, we beseech thee, O God of hosts: look down from heaven, and behold, and visit this vine; And the vineyard which thy right hand hath planted, and the branch that thou madest strong for thyself. It is burned with fire, it is cut down: they perish at the rebuke of thy countenance. (Psa 80:8-16)

The vine was brought out of Egypt (v8), so we can understand that the vine is a figure of Israel's Exodus. Notice how the rest of that passage tracks their journey from Egypt, their entry to the land of Canaan, and their establishment as a nation, in pictoral language similar to a parable.

The Psalm helps us understand other Scripture which uses the same symbols. Notice, for example, the vineyard in the Song of Solomon:

> *Look not upon me, because I am black, because the sun hath looked upon me: my mother's children were angry with me; they made me the keeper of the vineyards; but mine own vineyard have I not kept. (Sng 1:6)*

> *Solomon had a vineyard at Baalhamon; he let out the vineyard unto keepers; every one for the fruit thereof was to bring a thousand pieces of silver. My vineyard, which is mine, is before me: thou, O Solomon, must have a thousand, and those that keep the fruit thereof two hundred. (Sng 8:11-12)*

And Isaiah, speaking of Israel in the same way:

> *Now will I sing to my wellbeloved a song of my beloved touching his vineyard. My wellbeloved hath a vineyard in a very fruitful hill: And he fenced it, and gathered out the stones thereof, and planted it with the choicest vine, and built a tower in the midst of it, and also made a winepress therein: and he looked that it should bring forth grapes, and it brought forth wild grapes. (Isa 5:1-2)*

And finally, also the parables of Jesus, showing us that Jesus took his teaching straight from the Old Testament:

But what think ye? A certain man had two sons; and he came to the first, and said, Son, go work to day in my vineyard. He answered and said, I will not: but afterward he repented, and went. ... Hear another parable: There was a certain householder, which planted a vineyard... and let it out to husbandmen, and went into a far country: And when the time of the fruit drew near, he sent his servants to the husbandmen, that they might receive the fruits of it. And the husbandmen took his servants, and beat one, and killed another, and stoned another... But last of all he sent unto them his son, saying, They will reverence my son. But when the husbandmen saw the son, they said among themselves, This is the heir; come, let us kill him, and let us seize on his inheritance. And they caught him, and cast him out of the vineyard, and slew him ... And when the chief priests and Pharisees had heard his parables, they perceived that he spake of them. (Mat 21:28-29, 33-41, 45)

Food for thought

Verse 2 - These three tribes all resided on the West of the tabernacle (Num 2:18,20,22) so this is not an arbitrary grouping of three tribes.

Verse 13 - The wild beasts devouring the land echoes Leviticus 26:22.

Psalm 81

Listen!

> **Hear**, O my people, and I will testify unto thee: O Israel, if thou wilt **hearken** unto me; ... But my people would not **hearken** to my voice; and Israel would none of me. ... Oh that my people had **hearkened** unto me, and Israel had walked in my ways! (Psa 81:8, 11, 13)

The implication in these verses is that Israel wouldn't listen to who God was. He had declared Himself to them as the only God by saving them from Egypt with a mighty hand. But they gave the credit to a watered down version of God mixed up with ideas of the idols of other nations.

> There shall no strange god be in thee; neither shalt thou worship any strange god. I am the LORD thy God, which brought thee out of the land of Egypt... (Psa 81:9-10)

So in the next Psalm, we read "They do not know, nor do they understand".

> *They know not, neither will they understand; they walk on in darkness: all the foundations of the earth are out of course. (Psa 82:5)*

It's no coincidence that Jesus often repeated the phrase "he who has ears to hear, let him hear". Jesus was God's last and best attempt to reach His people. He showed them who He was by showing them His son. They should have listened but didn't.

We have the same choice to make:

> *See that ye refuse not him that speaketh. For if they escaped not who refused him that spake on earth, much more shall not we escape, if we turn away from him that speaketh from heaven... (Heb 12:25)*

Food for thought

Verse 7 - That Israel cried unto God when in Egypt is seen in Exo 2:23.

Verse 12 - The way that God is willing to give sinners up to their own foolish and evil desires is a chilling thought - may we order our lives so that we are never in the situation where God gives up on us.

"I gave them up" is quoted by Stephen in Acts 7:42, thus demonstrating that Israel's idolatry caused God to distance Himself from them. As Isaiah said, Israel's sins had separated them from Him (Isa 59:2).

Psalm 82

Defend the poor and fatherless

> A Psalm of Asaph. **God** standeth in the congregation of the **mighty**; he judgeth among the **gods**. (Psa 82:1)

In English, by and large, the word "god" always means the same to us — the Almighty creator. That's mostly because we've grown up with the word being used that way. In Scripture the word has a more nuanced meaning, as can be seen in the above verse. In Hebrew, the language used to write the original Bible, the word translated as "god" means "mighty". Given that God is the all-mighty, it is fittingly used of Him.

In this particular verse, we could read it like this:

> The **mighty** standeth in the congregation of the **mighty**; he judgeth among the **mighty**.

It makes a bit more sense like this rather than "he judgeth among the gods", because there is only one God.

The point I think being made by the Psalmist, is about the poor and needy:

Defend the poor and fatherless: do justice to the afflicted and needy. (Psa 82:3)

The poor and fatherless are not mighty, and have no-one mighty to stick up for them. They are in danger of being oppressed by those who are in power. So the Psalm tells us that in the congregation of the rulers and the powerful, among those who hold the lives of others in their hands, God will judge those who abuse their power to harm others.

With this in mind, perhaps the verse reads best like this:

***God** standeth in the congregation of the **mighty**; he judgeth among the**mighty**.*

Food for thought

Verse 6 - "Ye are Gods". Jesus' use of this verse in John 10:34 shows that the Psalmist is speaking of Israel's leaders. It seems that because of their exalted status they became proud and needed to be reminded of their mortality. A severe warning against pride.

Verse 8 - Jesus is the one who is to "inherit all nations" (see Psalm 2:8), as "all judgment" has been given to Jesus (John 5:22).

Psalm 83

Ten nations

There are ten nations that form a confederacy against Israel and say:

> Come, and let us cut them off from being a nation; that the name of Israel may be no more in remembrance. (Psalm 83:4)

Here are all ten listed, along with their ancestral origin according to Scripture.

Nation	Ancestor / Origin	Reference
Edom	Esau	Gen 25:30
Ishmaelites	Ishmael	Gen 17:20
Moab	Lot	Gen:19:37
Hagarites	Hagar (Egyptian)	Gen 16:15, 1Chron5:19, 1:31.
Gebal	*unknown*	Josh 13:5
Ammon	Lot	Gen:19:38
Amalek	Esau or earlier	Gen 14:7, 36:12
Philistia	Mizraim, son of Ham	Gen 10:6-14
Tyre	*unknown*	
Assyria	Nimrod	Gen 10:8-11

Food for thought

Verse 11 - The mention of Zeba and Zalmunna should send us back to the time of Gideon as spoken of in the book of Judges (see Judg 8:21).

Verse 18 - Notice that, whilst these nations have sought to destroy Israel, God's concern for them is that, rather than simply destroying them, they might turn to Him and recognise Him as God.

Psalm 84

Coming through the valley of weeping

> *My soul longeth, yea, even fainteth for the courts of the LORD:*
> *my heart and my flesh crieth out for the living God. (Psa 84:2)*

The Psalmist is describing strong feelings here. Perhaps he is in trouble and needs God to protect him. Perhaps he is fleeing and needs refuge. Whatever the cause, he wants to be with God, because he knows he will be safe when he is close to Him.

Further along the Psalm, verse 6 is rather cryptic:

> *Blessed is the man whose strength is in thee; in whose heart are the ways of them. Who passing through the valley of Baca make it a well; the rain also filleth the pools. (Psa 84:5-6)*

Looking up the word "Baca" in a Bible concordance we find it means "weeping", so we could suggest the verse reads:

"Blessed is the man whose strength is in thee… Who passing through the valley of weeping makes it a well of water"

Perhaps he is talking about the amount of tears, which are so many that they drench the ground? David went through this:

> *I am weary with my groaning; all the night make I my bed to swim; I water my couch with my tears. Mine eye is consumed because of grief; it waxeth old because of all mine enemies. Depart from me, all ye workers of iniquity; for the LORD hath heard the voice of my weeping. (Psa 6:6-8)*

Food for thought

Verse 4 - Jesus knew that those who "dwell" in God's house are blessed. This is why he encouraged Peter by telling him (and us) that he was going to prepare a place in God's house for us (see John 14:1-2).

Verse 11 - The promise that the upright will be blessed by God is seen also in Psalm 34:9-10.

Psalm 85

Turn away from folly

> To the chief Musician, A Psalm for the sons of Korah. LORD, thou hast been favourable unto thy land: thou hast brought back the captivity of Jacob. Thou hast forgiven the iniquity of thy people, thou hast covered all their sin. Selah. Thou hast taken away all thy wrath: thou hast turned thyself from the fierceness of thine anger. (Psa 85:1-3)

In the first three verses, it talks as if God has forgiven His people and restored them, but in v4 it is evident that this hasn't happened yet:

> Turn us, O God of our salvation, and cause thine anger toward us to cease. (Psa 85:4)

And in v5 the Psalmist asks:

> Wilt thou be angry with us for ever? Wilt thou draw out thine anger to all generations? (Psa 85:5)

So, the first three verses are a reflection of the trust that the writer has in the unchangeable nature of God — His forgiveness and mercy is not in question, and he therefore writes of it as if it has already happened. However, he recognises it is also a matter of whether the people were ready to turn away from their folly:

> *I will hear what God the LORD will speak: for he will speak peace unto his people, and to his saints: but* ***let them not turn again to folly****. (Psa 85:8)*

Food for thought

Verse 8 - Speaking peace is one of the characteristics of Jesus (see Zech 9:10) showing that this Psalm is Messianic (i.e. a prophecy of the Messiah).

Verse 10 - The way that "righteousness and peace" "kissed" shows that there is no conflict between mercy and truth. Once the truth has been established then the mercy of God can be shown correctly.

Psalm 86

God is ready to forgive

> For thou, Lord, art good, and **ready to forgive**; and plenteous in mercy unto all them that call upon thee. (Psa 86:5)

Do we see God as being ready to forgive? In other words, do we believe that He is predisposed to forgiveness, and waits for our confession?

Jesus spoke of this in his parable of the father who waited for his son to return:

> I will arise and go to my father, and will say unto him, Father, I have sinned against heaven, and before thee, And am no more worthy to be called thy son: make me as one of thy hired servants. And he arose, and came to his father. But **when he was yet a great way off, his father saw him, and had compassion**, and ran, and fell on his neck, and kissed him. (Luk 15:18-20)

It's a perfect example of someone "ready to forgive." This same father figure is used elsewhere in the Psalms to show that, as a father loves and pities his son, so our Father in Heaven pities us and is ready to show compassion when we fail:

> *He hath not dealt with us after our sins; nor rewarded us according to our iniquities. For as the heaven is high above the earth, so great is his mercy toward them that fear him. As far as the east is from the west, so far hath he removed our transgressions from us. Like **as a father pitieth his children, so the LORD pitieth them that fear him**. (Psa 103:10-13)*

Food for thought

Verse 11 - The Psalmist asks God to teach him His way. It is a good thing to ask God for instruction. However we do well to reflect on how He teaches. His instruction is there for us to read in His word, as it was for the Psalmist. The instruction comes from the Scriptures. They are able to make wise unto salvation (2Tim 3:16). So we should be praying that our eyes be opened to see things in the word (see Psa 119:18).

Verse 17 - We might think that the request that God would show David "a token" is the behaviour of a man who lacked faith. However, God specifically gave Abraham a token with the covenant of circumcision (Gen 17:11). When He told Moses that He would be with him when he went to Egypt God gave "a token" (see Exo 3:12).

Psalm 87

Dwelling in Zion

This Psalm is about being born in Zion. It tells us that God prefers Zion above every other place:

> The LORD loveth the gates of Zion more than all the dwellings of Jacob. (Psa 87:2)

Zion is even called the city of God in the next verse:

> Glorious things are spoken of thee, O city of God. Selah. (Psa 87:3)

While Zion sometimes appears to be used interchangeably with Jerusalem, it is important to understand that they are not one and the same. In 2Sam 5:7 we see that Zion is the City of David, the stronghold where he lived:

> Nevertheless David took the strong hold of Zion: the same is the city of David. (2Sa 5:7)

And in 2Chron 5:2 we see that the Ark of God actually dwelt there before it was placed in the Temple:

> *Then Solomon assembled the elders of Israel, and all the heads of the tribes, the chief of the fathers of the children of Israel, unto Jerusalem, to bring up the ark of the covenant of the LORD out of the city of David, which is Zion. (2Ch 5:2)*

So if God desires to dwell in Zion, was it therefore a backward step to take the Ark out of Zion to take it to the site of the temple?

In the promises to David in 2 Samuel 7 God gently rebukes David for wanting to build Him a house:

> *Go and tell my servant David, Thus saith the LORD, Shalt thou build me an house for me to dwell in? Whereas I have not dwelt in any house since the time that I brought up the children of Israel out of Egypt, even to this day, but have walked in a tent and in a tabernacle. In all the places wherein I have walked with all the children of Israel spake I a word with any of the tribes of Israel, whom I commanded to feed my people Israel, saying, Why build ye not me an house of cedar? (2Sa 7:5-7)*

If you read through the whole chapter with this Psalm in mind, you will notice that God implies He is already satisfied with where He is, living with David. The Ark was in the house of David, in Zion. God wants to dwell with men and women of faith, like David and like Jesus, and in this respect Zion has come to mean dwelling within the lineage and family of Jesus, the son of David.

Food for thought

Verse 4-5 - The idea of being born in Zion is developed in Galatians 4:26, where Jerusalem which is "above" is contrasted with the bondage of the law of Moses.

Verse 5 - When the Psalmist speaks of Jerusalem being "established" he is using a word associated with the promises to David (2Sam 7:12,16) and David's response (2Sam 7:25,26).

Psalm 88

Jonah's Psalm

Have you noticed how similar Psalm 88 is to Jonah's prayer in Jonah 2? How many links can you find? Do you think the Psalm was written with Jonah in mind? Here's one link, as an example:

> For **thou hadst cast me into the deep**, *in the midst of the seas; and the floods compassed me about: all thy billows and thy waves passed over me. (Jon 2:3)*

Like Jonah, the Psalmist knew God would hear his prayer even from the lowest pit of the earth:

> **Thou hast laid me** *in the lowest pit, in darkness,* **in the deeps.** *... Mine eye mourneth by reason of affliction: LORD, I have called daily upon thee, I have stretched out my hands unto thee. ... Shall thy wonders be known in the dark? and thy righteousness in the land of forgetfulness? (Psa 88:6, 9, 12)*

This prayer can apply to us too. No matter how low we get (in any way you wish to interpret 'low') God will still hear, and answer, if we pray honestly and contritely.

Is Psalm 89:1,9 this Psalmist's answer to prayer?

> *I will sing of the mercies of the LORD for ever: with my mouth will I make known thy faithfulness to all generations. ... Thou rulest the raging of the sea: when the waves thereof arise, thou stillest them. (Psa 89:1, 9)*

Food for thought

Verse 6 - A Psalm of the sons of Korah draws on the events of Korah's rebellion. Korah was destroyed when the earth opened and swallowed him up. What happened to him is used as a lesson in the New Testament a number of times. Jude 1:6 seems to draw on the darkness in the deep when he speaks of Korah's rebellion.

Verse 18 - Certainly David's friends and supporters forsook him when Absalom sought to take the throne. So maybe this is the historical basis for this Psalm?

Psalm 89

Who can calm the waves of the sea?

The calming of the waves shows the power and majesty of God:

> Thou rulest the raging of the sea: when the waves thereof arise, thou stillest them. (Psa 89:9)

It proves that the heavens and the earth, the whole world, is God's:

> The heavens are thine, the earth also is thine: as for the world and the fulness thereof, thou hast founded them. (Psa 89:11)

It means He is to be greatly reverenced by all those round Him:

> God is greatly to be feared in the assembly of the saints, and to be had in reverence of all them that are about him. (Psa 89:7)

But the Psalmist begins this with a question:

> For who in the heaven can be compared unto the LORD? who

among the sons of the mighty can be likened unto the LORD? (Psa 89:6)

When Jesus stilled the waves with just a word of command, he answered that question. Jesus is to be reverenced. Jesus is to be likened to God. Jesus has been given the world by his Father.

Jesus was like his Father, and when he stilled the waves he was showing the proof of his son-ship:

And he arose, and rebuked the wind, and said unto the sea, Peace, be still. And the wind ceased, and there was a great calm. ... And they feared exceedingly, and said one to another, What manner of man is this, that even the wind and the sea obey him? (Mar 4:39, 41)

The Psalm goes on to talk about those who know and accept that Jesus is the son of God:

Blessed is the people that know the joyful sound: they shall walk, O LORD, in the light of thy countenance. (Psa 89:15)

Food for thought

Verse 14 - The "justice and judgement" of this verse will be seen in the ruling Jesus (Isa 9:7) who will show the "mercy and truth" of God as seen in Exodus 34:6.

Verse 36 - This Psalm is an inspired commentary on the promises to David (see 2 Samuel 7 and 1 Chronicles 17). In speaking of "his seed" (v36), he links all servants of God with those promises which seem to be speaking of Solomon and Jesus.

IV

Psalms 90-106

Psalm 90

Threescore years and ten

Before the flood, men lived for approximately 1000 years, as we can see from the genealogy in Genesis 5:

> *And all the days of Methuselah were nine hundred sixty and nine years: and he died. ... And all the days of Lamech were seven hundred seventy and seven years: and he died. (Gen 5:27, 31)*

This may be what's being referred to in Psa 90:4:

> *For a thousand years in thy sight are but as yesterday when it is past, and as a watch in the night. (Psa 90:4)*

This seems to be confirmed because the Psalm seems to be in the context of the flood:

> *Thou carriest them away as with a flood; they are as a sleep: in the morning they are like grass which groweth up. (Psa 90:5)*

After the destruction made by the flood, this thousand year life expectancy gradually reduced to around 70 years, as mentioned in verse 10:

> *The days of our years are threescore years and ten; and if by reason of strength they be fourscore years, yet is their strength labour and sorrow; for it is soon cut off, and we fly away. (Psa 90:10)*

However, the writer of the Psalm is Moses (see v1), and he seems to be looking back at the wilderness journey of the children of Israel. Could it be that his comment about 70-80 years life expectancy is based on what he saw as the people wandered in the wilderness after they had refused to enter into the land of promise?

> *...All the people that came out of Egypt, that were males, even all the men of war, died in the wilderness by the way, after they came out of Egypt. ... For the children of Israel walked forty years in the wilderness, till all the people that were men of war, which came out of Egypt, were consumed, because they obeyed not the voice of the LORD: unto whom the LORD sware that he would not shew them the land, which the LORD sware unto their fathers that he would give us, a land that floweth with milk and honey. (Jos 5:4, 6)*

Food for thought

Note - Notice the contrast between these two Psalms of Moses. Psalm 90 focuses on the sins of the people and the judgement that God would bring. Psalm 91 focuses on the reward for the faithful. The immediate context is Joshua and Caleb.

Verse 4 - "A thousand years ... as yesterday" is quoted by Peter to show that God is not slack with respect to His promises (2 Peter 3:8). God had told those who refused to enter the land that they would perish in the wilderness - but almost 40 years passed before all these died. Why? Because He was looking for repentance (2 Peter 3:9).

Psalm 91

Under His wings shalt thou trust

For he shall give his angels charge over thee, to keep thee in all thy ways. They shall bear thee up in their hands, lest thou dash thy foot against a stone. (Psa 91:11-12)

These verses are quoted of Jesus in Luke 4:10-11, but the Psalm doesn't only look forward to Jesus, it also looks back at the example of others. Who does this phrase bring to mind?

He shall cover thee with his feathers, and under his wings shalt thou trust: his truth shall be thy shield and buckler. (Psa 91:4)

Verse 4 refers to Ruth 2:12 when Boaz requests God's care for Ruth, a widow and foreigner in a strange land:

The LORD recompense thy work, and a full reward be given thee of the LORD God of Israel, under whose wings thou art come to trust. (Rth 2:12)

And also David himself, the descendant of Ruth, uses the phrase when requesting help from God:

Keep me as the apple of the eye, hide me under the shadow of thy wings. (Psa 17:8)

Can you find any other places where the phrase "shelter under His wings" is used?

Also, can you think of anyone else in the Bible who might be mentioned in this Psalm, for example:

- verse 10 - No plague coming near their dwelling
- verse 13 - Overcoming the lion or the adder

Food for thought

Note - This Psalm (written by Moses) was given for the benefit of Joshua and Caleb. All of the promises relate to what they could expect in the wilderness. Because they had been faithful spies they would not die in the wilderness. However they would see their contemporaries all die off one by one in the wilderness. So read the Psalm and think of it being spoken to Joshua and Caleb. The language will then come alive. Then think about the promise that we ourselves have: "It is your Father's good pleasure to give you the kingdom" (Luke 12:32).

Verse 4-6 - Joshua and Caleb were certain that they would not die from any plague or battle in the wilderness – God had given his angel charge over them (91:11-12). In the same way Jesus was assured his Father's care but it did not give him license to take risks and tempt God.

Psalm 92

Dwelling in the house of the LORD

Praise ye the LORD. Praise ye the name of the LORD; praise him, O ye servants of the LORD. Ye that stand in the house of the LORD, in the courts of the house of our God. (Psa 135:1-2)

In Psalm 135, Israel is told to praise God. They were the nation that had been specially chosen by their calling out from Egypt and given the tabernacle in the wilderness. They were the one nation that could be said to stand in the house of the LORD, and in His courts, figuratively speaking.

But Hebrews 9 (see v24) tells us that the wilderness tabernacle was never actually the court of God at al:

For Christ is not entered into the holy places made with hands, **which are the figures of the true***; but into heaven itself, now to appear in the presence of God for us: (Heb 9:24)*

The tabernacle was merely an earthly representation. It was a figure, a similitude, a shadow of the real. A model, and the priests which served in it were likewise only representations of those who would minister in the *true* house of God.

The true house of God is a heavenly (i.e. spiritual) house. Jesus has gained entry to that house, and will ever be there, because God, whose house it is, lives forever (92:8):

> *But thou, LORD, art most high for evermore. (Psa 92:8)*

This house is not a shadow, but the real thing. In Psa 92:13 the wording from Psalm 135 is repeated:

> *Those that **be planted** in the house of the LORD **shall flourish** in the courts of our God. (Psa 92:13)*

It is talking about the faithful. In the next verse we are told that they will bear fruit in their old age. This is a reference to Abraham, the Father of the faithful:

> *They shall still **bring forth fruit** in old age; they shall be fat and flourishing. (Psa 92:14)*

So this is talking about here and now. Notice how closely these words relate to Psalm 1:

> *But his delight is in the law of the LORD; and in his law doth he meditate day and night. And he shall be like **a tree planted** by the rivers of water, that **bringeth forth his fruit in his season**; his leaf also **shall not wither**; and whatsoever he doeth shall prosper. (Psa 1:2-3)*

All the aspects of our Psalm are picked up there. The additional detail we learn now, ninety Psalms later on, is that to be planted in the word of God is to dwell in His courts.

Jesus says the same, when talking about his place in the house of his Father, and notice again that it is the word that we should be planted in:

> *I am the vine, ye are the branches: He that **abideth in me**, and I in him, the same **bringeth forth much fruit**: for without me ye can do nothing. ... If ye abide in me, and **my words abide in you**, ye shall ask what ye will, and it shall be done unto you. Herein is my Father glorified, that ye bear much fruit; so shall ye be my disciples. (Jhn 15:5, 7-8)*

Clearly there is a promise to us, now, if we are ready to search eagerly for it. It appears to be telling us that long life and vigour into old age are there as a gift from God to those whose lives are spent planted in His word. Abraham is portrayed to us as the perfect example of this:

> *For Sarah conceived, and bare Abraham a son in his old age, at the set time of which God had spoken to him. ... And Abraham was an hundred years old, when his son Isaac was born unto him. (Gen 21:2, 5)*
>
> *And Abraham was old, and well stricken in age: and the LORD had blessed Abraham in all things. (Gen 24:1)*
>
> *And these are the days of the years of Abraham's life which he lived, an hundred threescore and fifteen years. (Gen 25:7)*

And not only is there a promise for our mortal lives, but of course much more importantly for eternal life to come. This is ultimately what these scriptures are pointing to.

Food for thought

Verse 1 - The title of this Psalm tells us that it is "for the Sabbath day". Reading the Psalm we learn what God wanted His servants to do when they were freed from the worry and toil of labouring in the field. They were to "triumph in God's work" (verse 4). The fool does not understand the provision of a worry free life (verse 6). The lesson for us is whether we realise that we can devote ourselves to God's service in our lives because we know that he has provided for us (Matthew 6:8).

Verse 7 - "workers of iniquity", a phrase which occurs some 14 times in the Psalms, is not speaking about every man or woman who sins. It speaks of those who delight in iniquity; those who plan and continue in their iniquity.

Psalm 93

Explaining the symbol of the sea and the waves

> *The floods have lifted up, O LORD, the floods have lifted up their voice; the floods lift up their waves. The LORD on high is mightier than the noise of many waters, yea, than the mighty waves of the sea. (Psa 93:3-4)*

Do you think these verses are really talking about the sea and the waves, or about something else? How does the rest of the Bible use the phrase?

In Psalm 89 the raging of the waves is mentioned, but it is evident from the context that this is not talking about the literal waves:

> *Thou rulest the raging of the sea: when the waves thereof arise, thou stillest them. Thou hast broken Rahab in pieces, as one that is slain; thou hast scattered thine enemies with thy strong arm. (Psa 89:9-10)*

Later in the Psalm it speaks of the heavens, then explains that the heavens are a symbol for the assembly of the saints:

And the heavens shall praise thy wonders, O LORD: thy faithfulness also in the congregation of the saints. For who in the heaven can be compared unto the LORD? who among the sons of the mighty can be likened unto the LORD? God is greatly to be feared in the assembly of the saints, and to be had in reverence of all them that are about him. (Psa 89:5-7)

Likewise, the raging waves are connected with God "breaking Rahab in pieces", which is a phrase used of His victory over Egypt:

Awake, awake, put on strength, O arm of the LORD; awake, as in the ancient days, in the generations of old. Art thou not it that hath cut Rahab, and wounded the dragon? Art thou not it which hath dried the sea, the waters of the great deep; that hath made the depths of the sea a way for the ransomed to pass over? (Isa 51:9-10)

So, are the waves used as a symbol of the Gentile nations? I think so, and Ezekiel appears to make that point directly:

*Therefore thus saith the Lord GOD; Behold, I am against thee, O Tyrus, and **will cause many nations to come up against thee, as the sea causeth his waves to come up.** (Eze 26:3)*

So, what is our Psalm saying? It is written about the nations around Israel that have risen against her in battle, and of the LORD who is stronger than they, and has delivered her from all her enemies.

Food for thought

Verse 2 - That God is from everlasting is so obvious. However this truth is seen as a reason to praise God (Psalm 41:13, 106:48) and because of His everlasting nature, salvation is assured (Habakkuk 1:12). In a similar way, the fact that Jesus "ever liveth" (Hebrews 7:25) is the guarantee that our salvation is sure.

Verse 5 - In saying that God's testimonies are sure, the Psalmist is echoing the idea of Psalm 19:7. The fact that God's testimonies are sure has a consequence, but only for those who take heed to them. They are made wise!

Psalm 94

God, to whom vengeance belongs

This Psalm can be seen in the context of Saul slaying eighty five priests in 1Sam 22:18. At this time David was completely powerless to do anything to avenge this terrible crime. Thus he prays and writes this Psalm, addressing it to God like this:

> O LORD God, to whom vengeance belongeth... (Psa 94:1)

But Saul's crime didn't end at slaying the men. He went further than that. David notes:

> *They slay the widow and the stranger, and murder the fatherless.* (Psa 94:6)

The record in 1Sam 22:19 corroborates. It says this:

> *And Nob, the city of the priests, smote he with the edge of the sword, both men and women, children and sucklings, and oxen, and asses, and sheep, with the edge of the sword.* (1Sa 22:19)

This terrible crime happened because of Saul's hatred for David, and so David felt terrible personal regret. He wanted desperately to avenge the deaths of these innocent people — but Saul was God's anointed King, and while that was the case, David could do nothing to lay a finger on him. So he asks:

> *Who will rise up for me against the evildoers? or who will stand up for me against the workers of iniquity? (Psa 94:16)*

We too will have situations in our lives where we feel wickedness has gone unpunished. Jesus tells us to "turn the other cheek," for it is God who will make a reckoning with the wicked.

Food for thought

Verse 9-12 - God has the ability to be aware of all that we do, but this should not bring terror to our hearts. Rather it should help us to appreciate that our God is a God of love who has the desire for us to change our characters, and will help us do so.

Verse 12 - The word "blessed" here can be translated "happy". We might not think that we should be happy when God chastens us, but we should remember that God chastens those He loves (Prov 3:12, Heb 12:6).

Psalm 95

Will we ever see God?

Our hearts can be either hard like pottery, or malleable like clay. In verse 8 the reader is urged not to harden his heart as the children of Israel did. Why is the state of the heart so important? Why is it so vital that it yield, rather than remain unmoved?

> **Harden not your heart**, *as in the provocation, and as in the day of temptation in the wilderness: (Psa 95:8)*

Our aim as followers of Jesus Christ is to find God. It is He who has created us, and has the key to our continued existence. It is He who provides all things for our daily survival and well-being, just as He provided for Israel in the wilderness. Our aim is ultimately to enter into His presence, so that we can be with Him, and praise Him for His goodness in that provision to us:

> *Let us come before his presence with thanksgiving, and make a joyful noise unto him with Psalms. (Psa 95:2)*

But in Hebrews 12v9-14 we are told that no-one will see God, unless they yield to His chastening. Unless we allow ourselves to be moulded by the guidance and correction of God, we cannot be changed, we will never be **holy**, and therefore we will never be ready to enter His presence:

> *Furthermore we have had fathers of our flesh which corrected us, and we gave them reverence: shall we not much rather be in subjection unto the Father of spirits, and live? For they verily for a few days chastened us after their own pleasure; but he for our profit,* ***that we might be partakers of his holiness.*** *Now no chastening for the present seemeth to be joyous, but grievous: nevertheless afterward it yieldeth the peaceable fruit of righteousness unto them which are exercised thereby... Follow peace with all men, and* ***holiness, without which no man shall see the Lord:*** *(Heb 12:9-14)*

Psalm 94v12-13 calls those whom God chastens "blessed". And why?

> *"That thou mayest give him rest from the days of adversity"*

In the Kingdom we will rest, and God will rest. God is still at work in His creation. He is making a new creation in you and me, if we will let Him, and His creative work sometimes involves some adversity for our benefit. That rest from adversity is waiting for us, but first there is a little training and correction to be gone through. If we yield to it, and soften our hearts in humility, we will be trained by God to be holy, we will enter that rest, and we will see Him:

> *Blessed are the meek: for they shall inherit the earth. ... Blessed are the pure in heart: for they shall see God. (Mat 5:5, 8)*

The opposite also will be true. If we harden our hearts to it, try to avoid it, or refuse to learn from it, we're in danger of the same fate as the children of Israel (Psa 95:8,11, Heb 3:11-13, 4:11).

Food for thought

Verse 9 - In saying that Israel "proved" God we realise that they had learnt that God meant what He said — Numbers 14:23 — that they would not enter into the land. As if they needed further proof that God will keep His word! Clearly those at the border of the land for the first time did not believe what He had said.

Verse 7 - In speaking of the children of Israel as "sheep," the Psalmist is using an idea which is a clear Biblical theme. We see it in Ezekiel 34 as a warning to the leaders in Israel. We also see it in Jesus' teaching – for example Matthew 18:12.

Psalm 96

Sing a new song

> *O sing unto the LORD a new song: sing unto the LORD, all the earth. (Psa 96:1)*

The phrase "new song" is very important in the Old Testament. It often relates to the shift in national culture that Israel should have made, from an inward looking culture - of invading the land and keeping strangers out - to one of embracing Gentile converts and teaching them about God:

> *Declare his glory **among the heathen**, his wonders **among all people**. (Psa 96:3)*

It is a change in culture that the Jews never grasped; even at the time of Jesus they still thought it was their role to look down on foreigners as invaders. Ultimately, it was only when God cast out the Jews from His land that this new song was sung... without them.

See in this Psalm how many references there are to a new way of access to God for the Gentile nations. What other symbols, other than a song, does it use? Where else in the Bible can you find these?

Food for thought

Note - This Psalm is seen in its entirety, with slight differences, in 1Chron 16:23-33. This places this Psalm at the time of bringing the ark to Zion. Or at least it shows that the Psalm relates to that event.

Verse 13 - Paul (in Acts 17:31) quotes the work of God. From Acts we see the way in which God is going to judge the world is by Jesus Christ. All judgement has been given to the son (John 5:27).

Psalm 97

Ye that love the LORD, hate evil

> *The hills melted like wax at the presence of the LORD, at the presence of the Lord of the whole earth. (Psa 97:5)*

Verse 5 links this Psalm to the prophecy of Micah:

> *And the mountains shall be molten under him, and the valleys shall be cleft, as wax before the fire, and as the waters that are poured down a steep place. (Mic 1:4)*

The contexts of both passages are also similar, as both speak of judgements on idols and graven images:

> *Confounded be all they that serve graven images, that boast themselves of idols: worship him, all ye gods. (Psa 97:7)*

Notice that in this Psalm there is a clear distinction made between those that practice idolatry and those who hate it. God's presence, while bringing automatic judgement on some, means salvation to the other:

Ye that love the LORD, hate evil: he preserveth the souls of his saints; he delivereth them out of the hand of the wicked. (Psa 97:10)

Food for thought

Verse 2 - That God can be surrounded by darkness is seen elsewhere (Exodus 20:21, 1 Kings 8:12), but 1 John 1:5 says "God is light, and in Him is no darkness at all". Do you think the Bible contradicts itself or, if we read it carefully, is there a way to reconcile these statements?

Verse 7 - This verse gives us a contrast. Instead of the gods — idols — being worshipped, the "gods" that is the angels (see Hebrews 1:6) actually worship Jesus after his resurrection. So the correct relationship is shown. The idols are nothing, but to Jesus every knee shall bow.

Psalm 98

Jerusalem exalted above the hills

The occasion that fits this Psalm most clearly is the deliverance of Jerusalem at the time of Hezekiah. It was God Himself that saved His people, without any help from Hezekiah's army:

> O sing unto the LORD a new song; for he hath done marvellous things: his right hand, and his holy arm, hath gotten him the victory. (Psa 98:1)

It was following this miraculous victory that the whole of the surrounding peoples heard about it and sought Hezekiah:

> He hath remembered his mercy and his truth toward the house of Israel:**all the ends of the earth have seen the salvation of our God.** (Psa 98:3)

The account of Hezekiah and the invasion of Sennacherib is found in 2Chronicles 32, and the passage that sums up what we see in our Psalm is at the end of the account:

> *Thus the LORD saved Hezekiah and the inhabitants of Jerusalem from the hand of Sennacherib the king of Assyria, and from the hand of all other, and guided them on every side. And many brought gifts unto the LORD to Jerusalem, and presents to Hezekiah king of Judah: so that he was magnified in the sight of all nations from thenceforth. (2Ch 32:22-23)*

This incident and this Psalm look forward to another occasion in the future where God will again show His might in the earth at the return of Jesus. It will again be Jerusalem in trouble, and its deliverance that shows God's power to the whole world. At this time it will be Jesus, not Hezekiah, that will be set up as King reigning from Jerusalem and showing righteousness to the whole world:

> *But in the last days it shall come to pass, that the mountain of the house of the LORD shall be established in the top of the mountains, and it shall be exalted above the hills; and people shall flow unto it. And many nations shall come, and say, Come, and let us go up to the mountain of the LORD, and to the house of the God of Jacob; and he will teach us of his ways, and we will walk in his paths: for the law shall go forth of Zion, and the word of the LORD from Jerusalem. (Mic 4:1-2)*

Food for thought

Verse 3 - The way in which "He hath remembered his mercy" was in the provision of Jesus. See how these words are used by Mary in Luke 1:54.

Verse 9 - Judging the world in righteousness is seen on a number of occasions in Scripture (Psa 9:6, 96:3, Acts 17:31) which is in stark contrast with the judgement made by the world around us, which is too often skewed by greed and self interest.

Psalm 99

Intercessors

> ***Moses*** *and **Aaron** among his priests, and **Samuel** among them that call upon his name; they called upon the LORD, and he answered them. He spake unto them in the cloudy pillar: they kept his testimonies, and the ordinance that he gave them. Thou answeredst them, O LORD our God: thou wast a God that forgavest them, though thou tookest vengeance of their inventions. (Psa 99:6-8)*

Moses, Aaron and Samuel all interceded for Israel to keep them from being destroyed for their iniquity:

Moses: Numbers 14:10-24

Aaron: Numbers 16:41-50

Samuel: 1 Samuel 7:3-10

Food for thought

Verses 2,6,7 - In saying "sitteth between the cherubim" the Psalmist is reflecting on the promise of Exodus 29:45: "And I will dwell among the children of Israel, and will be their God." In mentioning the cloudy pillar (verse 7) there is another reference to tabernacle worship. However, the Psalm was certainly written after that time (see the reference to Samuel in verse 6), so worship in Zion (verse 2) must be talking about worship in the wilderness.

Verse 7 - As the record says that "He spake unto them in the cloudy pillar" and we know that the cloudy pillar was visible to Aaron and Moses, can we conclude also that it was still visible in Samuel's day?

Psalm 100

When all the earth will make a joyful noise

This Psalm goes together with the preceding Psalms to talk about how God's rule, and the gospel of salvation, would be extended to the Gentile nations:

> A Psalm of praise. *Make a joyful noise unto the LORD,* **all ye lands.** *(Psa 100:1)*

There are roughly four time periods in Scripture where we could say this happened or will happen.

1) During the early part of the reign of Solomon, when his wisdom gave him influence in the sight of all nations:

> *And Solomon's wisdom excelled the wisdom of all the children of the east country, and all the wisdom of Egypt. For he was wiser than all men; than Ethan the Ezrahite, and Heman, and Chalcol, and Darda, the sons of Mahol: and his fame was in* **all nations** *round about. (1Ki 4:30-31)*

2) During Hezekiah's reign, when the invading nation of Assyria was destroyed by God and Hezekiah's fame went out throughout the world:

*And many brought gifts unto the LORD to Jerusalem, and presents to Hezekiah king of Judah: so that he was magnified in the sight of **all nations** from thenceforth. (2Ch 32:23)*

3) After the death of Jesus, when the Kingdom was taken away from Israel and distributed instead to the Gentiles — in a spiritual sense only:

*And this gospel of the kingdom shall be preached in all the world for a witness unto **all nations**; and then shall the end come. (Mat 24:14)*

4) At the return of Jesus when he will reign from Jerusalem over all the world:

*Yet have I set my king upon my holy hill of Zion. I will declare the decree: the LORD hath said unto me, Thou art my Son; this day have I begotten thee. Ask of me, and I shall give thee **the heathen** for thine inheritance, **and the uttermost parts of the earth** for thy possession. (Psa 2:6-8)*

Food for thought

Verse 3 - The sheep of God's pasture (v3) should praise God because of His goodness. This contrasts starkly with the "sheep of His pasture" (Psalm 95:7) who complained at His provision in the wilderness.

Verse 5 - God's "mercy" and His "truth" are repeatedly seen together, for example Gen 24:27, Psa 25:10, 57:3, 61:7, 85:10, 86:15, 89:14 to list but a few.

Psalm 101

David removes the deceitful from his presence

> *He that worketh deceit shall not dwell within my house: he that telleth lies shall not tarry in my sight. (Psa 101:7)*

This Psalm is perhaps written at the start of David's reign and he is laying out his intentions. Chief among these is his intention to surround himself only with truth tellers, and to remove all liars from his presence.

This seems a wise course of action. Liars could not be trusted to give un-biased council, and for a king who would need to act on the recommendations of his inner circle, that could soon spell disaster.

But I wonder if he is thinking of someone specific here? Is there someone in David's life that has helped him make up his mind that he must under no circumstances allow such people near him?

Using a Strongs Concordance or online search program, and searching for the words "works deceit" (Strongs words H6213 and H7423) gives us a passage in Psalms that might shed some light on it:

> *Thy tongue deviseth mischiefs; like a sharp razor, working deceitfully. (Psa 52:2)*

In this passage David is clearly thinking of someone in particular, and notice that they are described in the same way as Psalm 101. If we look in the context we see the following:

> *To the chief Musician, Maschil, (A Psalm of David, when Doeg the Edomite came and told Saul, and said unto him, David is come to the house of Ahimelech.) (Psa 52:title)*

So there it is, right there in the introduction to the Psalm. Doeg the Edomite was the one that David is thinking about in Psalm 52, and by using the same wording in Psalm 101, the Scripture is giving us a clue that Doeg is being thought about again here.

Doeg was someone who was in Saul's inner circle, and it was his slanderous lies about David that caused the cruel deaths of many righteous men. You can read the account in 1 Samuel 21 and 22. David could be thinking of this cruel, lying man's slander when thinking about who to include in his own inner circle. David is intent on being a better King than Saul!

> *Whoso privily slandereth his neighbour, him will I cut off: him that hath an high look and a proud heart will not I suffer. (Psa 101:5)*

Food for thought

Verse 7 - David sets himself a high standard of life. To help him to achieve it he will keep good company. So he will not entertain "deceit" in his house. Whilst we may be very careful who we invite into our homes, are we so discerning about the things we watch on the TV or online, or the music and pod-casts we listen to?

Verse 6 - When David speaks of the one who "walketh in a perfect way," maybe he had in Mind Abraham who was called to walk in that way – Gen 17:1.

Psalm 102

Heavens and the earth: A key to prophetic Scripture

If we look at what is repeated in this Psalm, we get the impression the Psalm is about Zion. See v13,16,21.

> Thou shalt arise, and have mercy upon **Zion:** *for the time to favour her, yea, the set time, is come... When the LORD shall build up* **Zion***, he shall appear in his glory... To declare the name of the LORD in* **Zion***, and his praise in Jerusalem.* (Psa 102:13, 16, 21)

If this is the case, then this chapter can be used as a prophetic "key" for a phrase that crops up many times in Scripture: "The Heavens and the Earth."

If the context of this chapter is talking about Zion/Jerusalem, then the "heavens" and "earth" in v25-26 must be speaking about this too:

> *Of old hast thou laid the foundation of the* **earth:** *and the* **heavens** *are the work of thy hands. They shall perish, but thou shalt endure: yea, all of them shall wax old like a garment; as a*

vesture shalt thou change them, and they shall be changed. (Psa 102:25-26)

Let's form a hypothesis that the heavens and the earth in this chapter are Zion.

Lets break down this passage and see if our hypothesis fits:

"Of old hast thou laid the foundation of the earth: and the heavens are the work of thy hands."

God creating the nation of Israel, setting up laws, a ruling structure and religious structure. It is seen in this context in Zechariah, speaking of Israel:

*The burden of the word of the LORD for Israel, saith the LORD, which stretcheth forth the **heavens**, and layeth the foundation of the **earth**, and formeth the spirit of man within him. Behold, I will make **Jerusalem** a cup of trembling unto all the people round about, when they shall be in the siege both against Judah and against **Jerusalem**. (Zec 12:1-2)*

So, that part seems to fit. How about the second half?

"They shall perish, but thou shalt endure: yea, all of them shall wax old like a garment; as a vesture shalt thou change them, and they shall be changed"

This national structure would cease to be. Its law would be superseded and have no power. But God would endure, unchangeable.

This is seen in a similar context in Isaiah, this time speaking of the country of Edom:

*And all the host of **heaven** shall be dissolved, and the **heavens** shall be rolled together as a scroll: and all their host shall fall down, as the leaf falleth off from the vine, and as a falling fig from the fig tree. For my sword shall be bathed in **heaven**: behold, it shall come down upon Idumea, and upon the people of my curse, to judgment. (Isa 34:4-5)*

So, when Scripture uses the symbol of a heaven and earth, it seems to be talking about a nation and its ruling structure. It can apply to any nation, as we have seen here of both Israel and Edom. When it grows old and perishes this is perhaps the removal of the dominant philosophy or ruling structure guiding the nation.

When you see the heaven and earth mentioned elsewhere in Scripture, bear this chapter and its meaning in mind.

Food for thought

Verse 3 - If we wonder what the Psalmist is feeling, we can get some idea by looking at the similar phrase in Job 30:30 where Job speaks of his feelings.

Verse 16 - The appearance of God in glory will be seen in the return of the risen Christ (Colossians 3:4).

Psalm 103

The son's repentance and father's forgiveness

This Psalm reminds me of the parable of the lost son. It's a Psalm, perhaps *the* Psalm, about forgiveness. In v5 it says:

> Who satisfieth thy mouth with good things; so that thy youth is renewed like the eagle's. (Psa 103:5)

In Luke 15 vs 16 and 23 we see the hunger of the son being used to contrast the state of a man before and after he repents and returns to his father:

> And he would fain have filled his belly with the husks that the swine did eat: and no man gave unto him. ... And bring hither the fatted calf, and kill it; and let us eat, and be merry. (Luk 15:16, 23)

The parable paints a picture of complete forgiveness with no half measures, and it's the satisfying of hunger (by the preparation of the fatted calf) that confirms to us that his father has indeed forgiven him. In v13 of the Psalm, we similarly get the most wonderful reassurance of God's grace:

> *Like as a father pitieth his children, so the LORD pitieth them that fear him. (Psa 103:13)*

David's Illness

There are clues in this Psalm indicating that David suffered illness at the same time as struggling with the guilt of his sin of committing adultery with Bathsheba:

- v3 "who heals all your diseases"
- v4 "redeems your life from destruction"
- v5 "so that you youth is renewed"

This illness is never mentioned outright in the narrative part of the Bible, but alluded to more than once in the Psalms — keep an eye out as you read the Psalms and you may spot them.

Food for thought

Verse 3 - In saying that God "forgiveth all thine iniquities" the Psalmist is recalling God's assurance in Exodus 34:7.

Verse 10 - The Psalmist recognises that God has been merciful to him. This attitude is reflected (Ezra 9:13) by Ezra. The context in Ezra 9 shows that this is not simply a statement about our lives generally. Ezra had specific sins in mind when he echoes the words of the Psalmist.

Psalm 104

He laid the foundations of the earth

I find verse 5 quite instructive. All throughout history there has been debate about the earth; whether it is flat, or shaped like a dish, what is at the end of it, and whether one day it will fall off whatever it sits on. The questions are endless.

When we have no way of seeing, worries creep up on us. We wonder what might be beyond our horizon. Which is how it was until the day that aircraft were sent up into the sky, or perhaps hot air balloons, and eye witnesses for the first time saw the earth as a ball suspended in space. I find this verse wonderful because it doesn't seek to explain the unexplainable, and instead it just reassures us. God has laid the foundations of the earth so that it will never be removed, and perhaps that's the only thing we really *need* to know.

> *[the LORD] laid the foundations of the earth, that it should not be removed for ever. (Psa 104:5)*

Food for thought

Verse 4 - As this verse is used in Hebrews 1:7 and 14, we should reflect on the way in which God works in our lives through the angels. They are "ministering spirits, sent forth to minister for them who shall be heirs of salvation."

Verse 6-9 - Here the Psalmist makes a number of references to the flood narrative:

- Above the mountains (Genesis 7:19)
- At thy rebuke (Genesis 8:1)
- Cover the earth (Genesis 9:11)

Psalm 105

What is the result of faith in the promises?

For he remembered his holy promise, and Abraham his servant. (Psa 105:42)

The key point to remember in this chapter is that in verse 42 the writer comes back to the promise to Abraham which he introduces in v8-11:

He hath remembered his covenant for ever, the word which he commanded to a thousand generations. Which covenant he made with Abraham, and his oath unto Isaac; And confirmed the same unto Jacob for a law, and to Israel for an everlasting covenant: Saying, Unto thee will I give the land of Canaan, the lot of your inheritance. (Psa 105:8-11)

So all that happened to Israel, as outlined in-between (verses 12-41), is *because of those promises*. A similar point is made for us in Hebrews 11, showing that the promises engendered all these amazing acts of faith:

*By faith Abraham, when he was tried, offered up Isaac: and he that had **received the promises** offered up his only begotten son ... Who through faith subdued kingdoms, wrought righteousness, **obtained promises**, stopped the mouths of lions. (Heb 11:17, 33)*

Food for thought

Verse 15 - The mention of prophets clearly speaks of Abraham (Gen 20:7) when God reproved a king (Gen 20:5).

Verse 28-36 - Have you noticed that the plagues of the Exodus are ordered differently in this Psalm? Why do you think this might be?

Psalm 106

A prayer echoed through Israel's history

We have sinned with our fathers, we have committed iniquity, we have done wickedly. (Psalm 106:6)

I think the particular historical setting for this Psalm being written could be at the time of Hezekiah's reformations, which were done in the setting of the recent captivity of the Northern part of Israel. You can see evidence of this in Psa 106:47, which appears to mention the captivity:

Save us, O LORD our God, and gather us from among the heathen, to give thanks unto thy holy name, and to triumph in thy praise. (Psalm 106:47)

Compare the wording of v6 with the Chronicles account of the start of Hezekiah's reign:

For our fathers have trespassed, and done that which was evil in the eyes of the LORD our God, and have forsaken him, and have turned away their faces from the habitation of the LORD, and turned their backs. (2 Chronicles 29:6)

There are plenty of other places in the history of Israel where this phrase is used though, and the Psalm is a summary of many of the times Israel rebelled.

It is not long after Hezekiah's reformations that Judah falls back to idolatry and wickedness, and God causes them to go into captivity to Babylon. Here, after 70 years, Daniel prays to God, confessing their sins and the sins of their fathers as Hezekiah had done. Notice the precise quote from our Psalm:

> **We have sinned, and have committed iniquity, and have done wickedly**, *and have rebelled, even by departing from thy precepts and from thy judgments ... O Lord, to us belongeth confusion of face, to our kings, to our princes, and* **to our fathers**, *because* **we have sinned** *against thee ... Yea, all Israel have transgressed thy law, even by departing, that they might not obey thy voice; therefore the curse is poured upon us, and the oath that is written in the law of Moses the servant of God, because* **we have sinned** *against him ... And now, O Lord our God, that hast brought thy people forth out of the land of Egypt with a mighty hand, and hast gotten thee renown, as at this day;* **we have sinned, we have done wickedly.** *(Daniel 9:5, 8, 11, 15)*

So, we know that Daniel had this Psalm in mind and used it as a basis for his prayer, a prayer that was effective in that it was answered by an angel.

We also can (and should) use Psalms and other Scripture as the basis for our prayers. They can only be more effective if we make the effort to understand and then use the wording God has given us to use.

Food for thought

Verse 8 - We must resist the temptation to think that God saves because of our status. He saved Israel for "His name's sake."

Verse 30-31 - The mention of Phinehas quotes the events of Numbers 25 where he stayed the plague by killing the Midianitish woman and the Israelite leader. In that "it was counted to him for righteousness" (Psalm 106:31) he is like Abraham (Genesis 15:6) whose faith was counted to him for righteousness. Phinehas' faith was seen in the way he behaved.

V

Psalm 107-150

Psalm 107

Oh that men would praise the LORD for His goodness!

Oh that men would praise the LORD for his goodness, and for his wonderful works to the children of men! (Psalm 107:8)

This wonderful Psalm is split up into five sections plus an introduction and summary. Any of the five sections might relate to some incident in our lives where we have been graciously helped by the LORD when we thought hope was lost.

If we have had occasions like this then we need to ask ourselves the question:

"Did I thank the LORD for His goodness and wonderful works?"

Food for thought

Verse 6, 13, 19, 28 - Notice the repeated refrain that the people "cry" to God. On each occasion God delivered His people. Rather like the period of the Judges. Do we believe that God will hear our cries?

Verse 20 - The way in which the Psalmist speaks of God sending His word to produce healings is seen to have a fulfilment in the healing of the Centurion's servant in Matt 8:8.

Psalm 108

Why did David go to fight Edom?

In this Psalm David appears to be gearing up to fight Edom:

> *Who will bring me into the strong city? who will lead me into Edom? (Psalm 108:10)*

Genesis tells us that the Edomites were the descendants of Esau, the brother of Jacob whose name was changed to Israel:

> *And Esau said to Jacob, Feed me, I pray thee, with that same red pottage; for I am faint: therefore was his name called **Edom**. (Genesis 25:30)*

Why would David be fighting Israel's brethren?

The answer is that David could have been the man mentioned in a prophecy given by Balaam:

> *I shall see him, but not now: I shall behold him, but not nigh: there shall come a Star out of Jacob, and a Sceptre shall rise out of Israel, and shall smite the corners of Moab, and destroy all*

> the children of Sheth. **And Edom shall be a possession**, Seir also shall be a possession for his enemies; and Israel shall do valiantly. Out of Jacob shall come he that shall have dominion, and shall destroy him that remaineth of the city. (Numbers 24:17-19)

So David was most probably that "star" with a sceptre (i.e. a King) that would come from Israel and strike Moab and Edom.

This prophecy appears to talk about the "strong city" mentioned in our Psalm:

> Out of Jacob shall come he that shall have dominion, and **shall destroy him that remaineth of the city**.

So the question is, was David, the King of Israel, preparing to carry out God's prophetic judgement on the nation of Edom?

Food for thought

Verse 3 - In wishing to sing praise because of his victory over the nations David is not glorying in battle. His desire to sing praise is because God has worked in his life to deliver him. The battles won are all part of the development of the kingdom of God on earth at that time.

Verse 7 - When God speaks "in His holiness," He is speaking as one who is separate from the world and all things in it. The word "holy" means "separate". He stands, therefore, as the judge who is not prejudiced by human emotions.

Psalm 109

In response to my love, they are my adversaries

They compassed me about also with words of hatred; and fought against me without a cause. For my love they are my adversaries: but I give myself unto prayer. And they have rewarded me evil for good, and hatred for my love. (Psalm 109:3-5)

When former friends treat you with contempt without cause, it's extremely hard to bear. When you have shown them love and they throw it back in your face, it's difficult not to respond to their cursing with some of your own. But David turned his bitter words into prayer instead:

For my love they are my adversaries: but I give myself unto prayer. (Psalm 109:4)

Jesus did this too, in the garden of Gethsemane. An earlier Psalm, prophecying of Jesus as well as speaking David's heart at the time, tells us how brokenhearted these men were after the reproach of their loved ones who had turned against them.

> I am become a stranger unto my brethren, and an alien unto my mother's children. For the zeal of thine house hath eaten me up; and the reproaches of them that reproached thee are fallen upon me. When I wept, and chastened my soul with fasting, that was to my reproach...
>
> **Reproach hath broken my heart**; and I am full of heaviness: and I looked for some to take pity, but there was none; and for comforters, but I found none. (Psalm 69:8-10,20)

What can we learn from this? To pray rather than to respond angrily. If they could do it while broken hearted, surely we can do it with our small, daily, upsets?

Food for thought

Verse 8 - This Psalm is prayer for the overthrow of the counsel of Ahithophel who, along with Absalom, sought to overthrow the throne of David toward the end of his life. As such Ahithophel stands as a pattern of Judas, who betrayed Jesus. So we have the betrayal of two of the Lord's anointed ones. This is why the Psalm is quoted in the New testament and applied to Judas (see Acts 1:20). As we read the Psalm we therefore learn of David's feelings at this time and can gain an insight into how Jesus felt at the betrayal of his "familiar friend," Judas (see Psa 41:9).

Verse 26-27 - Whilst this Psalm clearly speaks of David's feelings towards Ahithophel, we must not see this as simply David seeking revenge. His concern is that people realise that all the things that happen to Ahithophel will be God's judgment.

Psalm 110

The beheaded heifer

> *He shall drink of the brook in the way: therefore shall he lift up the head. (Psalm 110:7)*

What does this verse mean? It is in the context of verse 6, which speaks of dead bodies:

> *He shall judge among the heathen, he shall fill the places with the dead bodies; he shall wound the heads over many countries. (Psalm 110:6)*

I think it could be a reference to Deuteronomy, where a heifer is slain by cutting off its head. This is done in a valley with water, hence the reference also to the brook in v7:

> *And the elders of that city shall bring down the heifer unto a rough valley, which is neither eared nor sown, and shall strike off the heifer's neck there in the valley: And the priests the sons of Levi shall come near; for them the LORD thy God hath chosen to minister unto him, and to bless in the name of the LORD; and*

> by their word shall every controversy and every stroke be tried: And all the elders of that city, that are next unto the slain man, shall **wash their hands over the heifer that is beheaded in the valley.** (Deuteronomy 21:4-6)

This is not where the similarities end. The reason for the heifer being offered in this (rather gruesome) way, is because a tragedy has happened:

> If one be found slain in the land which the LORD thy God giveth thee to possess it, lying in the field, and it be not known who hath slain him. (Deuteronomy 21:1)

Clearly a murder has taken place, yet there is no way of bringing the perpetrator to justice. The slaying of the heifer is a way of atoning for the innocent blood that has been shed:

> And they shall answer and say, Our hands have not shed this blood, neither have our eyes seen it. Be merciful, O LORD, unto thy people Israel, whom thou hast redeemed, and lay not innocent blood unto thy people of Israel's charge. **And the blood shall be forgiven them. So shalt thou put away the guilt of innocent blood from among you,** when thou shalt do that which is right in the sight of the LORD. (Deuteronomy 21:7-9)

So, having looked at the context of the heifer in Deuteronomy, what is the application to this Psalm?

I think the Psalm is prophetic of the return of Jesus as King to the earth. In the mighty battles that will take place with those who resist his Kingship, there will, according to this and other prophecies, be many slain:

The Lord at thy right hand shall strike through kings in the day of his wrath. (Psalm 110:5)

The reference to Deuteronomy could be there to show that Jesus will be innocent of their blood.

Perhaps, more than that. Jesus was the man who would be slain outside the city, as a totally innocent man, and yet the "kings of the earth" were the ones who killed him. This seems to be speaking of justice finally being carried out for the crime of that murder.

The key to understanding this is to recognise that Israel put Jesus to death, and under the law of Moses were guilty because their hands *did* shed his blood, their eyes *did* see it, and therefore the guilt *was* laid to their charge:

> *And they shall answer and say,* **Our hands** *have not* **shed this blood***, neither have* **our eyes seen it***. Be merciful, O LORD, unto thy people Israel, whom thou hast redeemed, and lay not innocent blood unto thy people of Israel's charge. And the blood shall be forgiven them. (Deuteronomy 21:7-8)*

Food for thought

Note - The promise of the son to David, and David bringing the ark to Zion are closely related. This is probably the most quoted Psalm in the New Testament. It has its origins in the time when David brought the ark to Zion. For at that time David officiated as a priest after the order of Melchisedec in the way that he gave bread and wine to the people (1 Chronicles 16:3) and wore priestly garments (2 Samuel 6:14) and offered sacrifices (2 Samuel 6:17). At this time David "sat before the Lord" (2 Samuel 7:18).

Verse 6 - Jesus will "judge among the heathen" at the time that the kingdom is established. This judgment will continue into the kingdom when, for example, judgment will be made on nations that decide not to go to Jerusalem annually to keep the feast of Tabernacles – Zech 14:18.

Psalm 111

Wisdom starts somewhere, but it doesn't finish there

> *The fear of the LORD is the beginning of wisdom: a good understanding have all they that do his commandments: his praise endureth for ever. (Psalm 111:10)*

The first part of this is repeated in several proverbs,

> *The fear of the LORD is the beginning of knowledge: but fools despise wisdom and instruction. (Proverbs 1:7)*

> *The fear of the LORD is the beginning of wisdom: and the knowledge of the holy is understanding. (Proverbs 9:10)*

But the specific slant here is that, not only is the fear of the LORD the *beginning* of wisdom, keeping His commandments will *grow* that wisdom. To see an example of this, we have only to look at the context of the Psalm, which is Israel's possession of the land of Canaan:

He hath shewed his people the power of his works, that he may give them the heritage of the heathen. The works of his hands are verity and judgment; **all his commandments are sure. They stand fast for ever and ever**, *and are done in truth and uprightness. He sent redemption unto his people: he hath commanded his covenant for ever: holy and reverend is his name. (Psalm 111:6-9)*

To see an example of the truth of these words, we can consider the long lasting nature of the laws concerning public health. In the wilderness God gave them a law which thousands of years before its time kept disease at bay by washing of hands, safe disposal of waste, and isolation of infectious cases.

Food for thought

Verse 3 - God's work is "honourable". Since we should reflect His character, are all the things we do honourable?

Verse 10 - We might think that "the fear of the Lord" is the language of Solomon (Proverbs 1:7 9:10), but it has its origin - in principle - in Deuteronomy 4:6 and the Psalmist develops it here. The one who fears the Lord will keep His commandments and thus will be "wise".

Psalm 112

Giving to the poor and allowing God to reimburse

> *He hath dispersed, he hath given to the poor; his righteousness endureth for ever; his horn shall be exalted with honour. (Psa 112:9)*

Notice in verse 9 the phrase "He hath dispersed, he hath given to the poor." This phrase is quoted in 2 Corinthians 9:9, and matching the two chapters together is quite instructive.

In the Corinthians passage we are being told that we can safely spend everything in working for the good of others, because God will ensure we don't go without:

> *And God is able to make all grace abound toward you; that ye, always having all sufficiency in all things, may abound to every good work: As it is written, He hath dispersed abroad; he hath given to the poor: his righteousness remaineth for ever. (2Co 9:8-9)*

Then in the next verse it quotes the Psalm. So how could the writer to the Corinthians get that conclusion from this Psalm?

Take a look at verse 5:

> *A good man sheweth favour, and lendeth: he will guide his affairs with discretion. (Psa 112:5)*

And notice that this is followed with:

> *Surely he shall not be moved ... He shall not be afraid of evil tidings. (Psa 112:6-7)*

Putting ourselves in the shoes of those living in Old Testament times, where there was no government provision for the poor, giving our goods away could bring very real concerns for our welfare. This means that only those who had faith in the power of God could give liberally. Thus "he shall not be afraid" is the faith that causes the work (lending) to happen.

Do we believe the Psalm and the Corinthians passage, and do we believe in God's power to reimburse?

Food for thought

Verse 4 - That God is gracious and full of compassion has already been revealed to Moses – Exodus 34:6-7. The Psalmist can have confidence in God, because He has already revealed Himself. We, likewise, can take comfort.

Verse 10 - The gnashing with the teeth that the Psalmist speaks of is not a literal activity that the wicked do towards the good. This is how the Jewish leaders would react to Stephen – Acts 7:54– when they were "cut to the heart" – another metaphor to speak of their emotions.

Psalm 113

Hannah's prayer

Verses v3-7 are taken from Hannah's prayer in 1Sam 2:1-10:

> *From the rising of the sun unto the going down of the same the LORD'S name is to be praised. The LORD is high above all nations, and his glory above the heavens. Who is like unto the LORD our God, who dwelleth on high, Who humbleth himself to behold the things that are in heaven, and in the earth! He raiseth up the poor out of the dust, and lifteth the needy out of the dunghill. (Psa 113:3-7)*

The Psalm then adds this lovely detail:

> *He maketh the barren woman to keep house, and to be a joyful mother of children. Praise ye the LORD. (Psa 113:9)*

Food for thought

Note - This Psalm presents a wonderful contrast. The creator of the universe humbles Himself that He might elevate those who are of "low degree". His son was involved in this for our sakes, in taking the form of a servant (Philippians 2:7). Do we appreciate the majesty of what our God has done for us?

Verse 5 - In asking "who is like unto the Lord our God" the Psalmist echoes the words of Exodus 15:11, which wer spoken joyously because of the overthrow of the Egyptians.

Psalm 114

God's presence during the Exodus from Egypt

Here are some references to the parts of Scripture this Psalm is talking about.

Verse 1 refers to the Exodus from Egypt (see Exodus 12):

> *When Israel went out of Egypt, the house of Jacob from a people of strange language. (Psa 114:1)*

Verse 3 refers to the parting of the red sea (Exodus 14) and of the Jordan (Joshua 3):

> *The sea saw it, and fled: Jordan was driven back. (Psa 114:3)*

Verse 7 refers to Deuteronomy 2:4 and Judges 5:4:

> *Tremble, thou earth, at the presence of the Lord, at the presence of the God of Jacob; (Psa 114:7)*

Verse 8 refers to Exodus 17:6 and Numbers 20:8:

Which turned the rock into a standing water, the flint into a fountain of waters. (Psa 114:8)

Food for thought

Verse 1-3 - This speaks of the Exodus of Israel from Egypt and their entry into the land of Canaan. So when we read of the earth trembling (v7), it speaks of the inhabitants of Canaan whose fear is exemplified by Rahab in Joshua 2:9-10.

Verse 1 - The use of the phrase "strange language" shows that the time in Egypt was a fulfilment of the curses of Deuteronomy 28:49.

Psalm 115

Three Psalms that overlap

There are three Psalms that mention the House of Aaron, and all of them have other similarities. If we read them together we get a fuller picture of the theme David is developing in these Psalms. Here is a quick summary of the overlap in content, but you will be able to see many more instances yourself.

Trust:

> Their idols... They that make them are like unto them; so is every one that **trusteth** in them. O Israel, **trust** thou in the Lord. (Psalm 115)

> It is better to **trust** in the Lord than to put confidence in man... All nations compassed me about. (Psalm 118)

> the idols ... They that make them are like unto them: so is every one that **trusteth** in them. (Psalm 135)

The house of Aaron:

> *He will bless the house of Israel; He will bless **the house of Aaron**. (Psalm 115)*

> *Let **the house of Aaron** now say, that His mercy endureth for ever. (Psalm 118)*

> *Bless the Lord, O house of Israel: bless the Lord, O **house of Aaron**. (Psalm 135)*

Food for thought

Verse 1-2 - In speaking of glory being given to God and not man (v1-2) and then speaking about man's idols (v18) we see that God is telling us that those who make idols are, in fact, seeking honour for themselves.

Verse 14 - The promise of an increase in children is an indication that the promise to Abraham was going to be fulfilled in them "I will make of thee a great nation" (Gen 12:2).

Psalm 116

How God trained David

In Psalm 116 David is greatly distressed. He calls out to the LORD in his trouble, and the LORD delivers him. There are some clues as to what the trouble was in verses 3 and 11. In v11 David uses the word "haste":

I said in my haste, All men are liars. (Psalm 116:11)

The only place where this word occurs in the history of David is in 1Sam 23:26, where David hasted to get away from Saul:

And Saul went on this side of the mountain, and David and his men on that side of the mountain: and David made haste to get away for fear of Saul; for Saul and his men compassed David and his men round about to take them. (1 Samuel 23:26)

It was on this occasion that Saul's armies completely surrounded David, and were about to capture and kill him. In verse 3 of the Psalm David says "the pains of Death have surrounded me", so it is likely that these two passages are a match:

The sorrows of death compassed me, and the pains of hell gat hold upon me: I found trouble and sorrow. (Psalm 116:3)

Being surrounded by an army intent on killing you is no easy deal. This meant certain death. God had allowed David to fall into the hands of his captor, but why? What was so important to God, that He was prepared to allow His servant David to go through such a dreadful trauma in order to achieve it? After he was saved from the situation, David says:

I love the LORD, because he hath heard my voice and my supplications. Because he hath inclined his ear unto me, therefore will I call upon him as long as I live. (Psalm 116:1-2)

Somehow, by these traumas, God had trained David to love and trust Him. And that was worth it.

Food for thought

Verse 1-2 - We all know how much we appreciate people talking to us and taking notice of what we say. Our God is like that. Prayer is the way we communicate with Him and reading His word is how we hear Him speaking to us.

Verse 16 - The statement "I am the son of thy handmaid" may refer to Ruth, but looks forward to Jesus and Mary - his mother. It is Jesus who, in the ultimate sense, offered "the sacrifice of thanksgiving" (see verse 17).

Psalm 117

If only they had read this properly

If we take the last verse of the previous Psalm as context, we can conclude that Psalm 117 is about the LORD's house in Jerusalem. If we make that connection, it tells us that that house was supposed to be the central place for worship for the Gentiles. We could rearrange the order of these verses and write the Psalm like this just to emphasise that point:

Psalm 116:19 - 117:2 (rearranged)

> *O praise the Lord In the courts of the Lord's house, in the midst of thee, O Jerusalem. Praise ye the Lord,* **all ye nations:** *praise him, all ye people. For his merciful kindness is great toward us: and the truth of the Lord endureth for ever. Praise ye the Lord.*

If the Scribes and Pharisees had made these connections they would not have killed Jesus, stoned Stephen, or put Paul in jail. Don't ever let anyone tell you that a correct and precise interpretation of Old Testament Scripture is unimportant!

Food for thought

Note - This short Psalm gives us the reason why we should worship God - He is kind towards us!

Verse 2 - The "merciful kindness" of which David speaks is something which Solomon recognised about the way that God dealt with his father (1 Kings 3:6).

Psalm 118

They compassed me about

There is a significant detail in verses 10-12. Four times David uses the word "compassed", repeating it over and over again to emphasise its significance. What could he be referring to?

> All nations **compassed** me about: but in the name of the LORD will I destroy them. They **compassed** me about; yea, they **compassed** me about: but in the name of the LORD I will destroy them. They**compassed** me about like bees; they are quenched as the fire of thorns: for in the name of the LORD I will destroy them. (Psalm 118:10-12)

In 1Sam 22:17-18,20, speaking of the dreadful act of mass murder that Saul and Doeg perpetrated, we find that the same Hebrew word is again used four times.

> And the king said unto the footmen that stood about him, **Turn**, and slay the priests of the LORD; because their hand also is with David, and because they knew when he fled, and did not shew

> it to me. But the servants of the king would not put forth their hand to fall upon the priests of the LORD. And the king said to Doeg, **Turn** thou, and fall upon the priests. And Doeg the Edomite **turned**, and he fell upon the priests, and slew on that day fourscore and five persons that did wear a linen ephod... And David said unto Abiathar, I knew it that day, when Doeg the Edomite was there, that he would surely tell Saul: I have **occasioned** the death of all the persons of thy father's house. (1 Samuel 22:17-18, 22)

This small detail leads me to believe that David is especially thinking of this event when writing Psalm 118. It was soon after this event that Saul started closing in on David:

> And Saul went on this side of the mountain, and David and his men on that side of the mountain: and David made haste to get away for fear of Saul; for Saul and his men **compassed David and his men round about** to take them. (1 Samuel 23:26)

Food for thought

Verse 6 - This verse, also quoted in Hebrews 13:6, shows the confidence that Jesus had during his life - right up until his death. So, like the recipients of the letter to the Hebrews, we should have the same confidence.

Verse 8 - Here the Psalmist voices a recurring theme in Scripture – that man cannot be relied upon – Psa 146:3, Isa 31:3, Jer 17:5.

Psalm 119:1-40

How to deal with sinful thoughts

Let's imagine you have a problem with chocolate. If there's some in the cupboard you can bet your life you'll have eaten it by the time the day is out. And your problem is causing you to gain a lot of weight. How do you deal with that kind of compulsion? If you tell yourself every few minutes not to think about chocolate, would that make it any better, or worse?

Sin seems a bit like that. Sometimes the more we try not to think sinful thoughts, the more they come to us.

The Psalm gives us a radical alternative to willpower. Take a look at these:

Ps 119:2-3

> "Blessed are they that keep his testimonies, and that seek him with the whole heart. They also do no iniquity."

Ps 119:9

> "Wherewithal shall a young man cleanse his way? by taking

heed thereto according to thy word."

Ps 119:11

"Thy word have I hid in mine heart, that I might not sin against thee."

Notice that in each case, it is suggested that a preoccupation with the word of God will automatically lead to a lack of sin. It is a radical upending of traditional thinking. Taking the chocolate analogy again, it is analogous to someone falling in love with a sport and in their pursuit of mastery, the exercise and fitness having the side effect of keeping their weight healthy.

This is worth thinking about further. As a Christian do we beat ourselves up over sin? Are we preoccupied with our own failings? Or, instead, are we in love with God's word, striving to learn and master it, so that in time our appetite for sin diminishes and all but disappears?

Food for thought

Verse 4 - Keeping the precepts "diligently" catches the exhortation of Deuteronomy 6:7.

Verse 9 - The answers as to how a young man should cleanse his ways are given by Jesus (John 15:3). The disciples were made clean through Jesus' words, which mirrors David's conclusions.

Psalm 119:41-80

The wonderful liberty given by God's precepts

And I will walk at liberty: for I seek thy precepts. (Psalm 119:45)

What do you think about verse 45? Do you think that the precepts of God give us liberty?

For example, how does "don't do any work on the Sabbath" give us liberty? If we worked an extra day in the week, we'd earn more, and be able to afford more things to make our lives easier.

Is that the way David looks at it? How about our friends, children or spouse — what do they think about it? Would they prefer to have us spend relaxed time with them, or be away at work seven days a week?

Perhaps God's law gives a balance that's been worked out carefully so that we don't have to work it out for ourselves? Perhaps the precepts of God give liberty because they save problems, stress, strain, anxiety and heartache in the long-run? Is one day spent with our family worth investing for better relationships in the long run? If that's the case then a national holiday every Sabbath is a wonderful idea, and if the Sabbath is a wonderful idea then perhaps the rest of the law is great advice too?

But of course that's looking at the Bible from our Western perspective only. Elsewhere in the world and throughout history people have been forced to work 7 days a week without a break. For those, the law of the Sabbath is a wonderful liberty.

In the new testament, a crowd gathered to hear Jesus, and he told them this:

> *Blessed are the poor in spirit: for theirs is the kingdom of heaven... Blessed are they which do hunger and thirst after righteousness: for they shall be filled (Matt 5:3-6).*

Jesus thought that the liberty of God's precepts was best appreciated by the poor, meek and hungry.

Food for thought

Verse 48 - The lifting up of hands is an idea used in the context of worship – Psalm 141:2– so we see David not only keeps God's commandments; He praises them. Do we hold God's teachings in Scripture in such a high regard?

Verse 62 - Praying "at midnight" is seen also in Paul and Silas (Acts 16:25).

Psalm 119:81-120

Words that live forever

David wants to show us that every part of his life, and by implication every part of ours, may be lived by recourse to God's word. He demonstrates it in spectacular fashion by writing 176 statements proving it! Testimonies, testament, commandments, statutes, judgements, precepts, ordinances, Gods word, and His law appear in just about every verse, yet every verse is different!

I think v89 is key to what David is getting across:

> *For ever, O LORD, thy word is settled in heaven. (Psalm 119:89)*

Many of the verses talk about earthly things or people passing away, whilst David trusts in, and is anchored by, the word of God.

Many verses talk about choosing that word, though mocked and despised because of it (for example, verses 19, 23, 39, 42, 46, 51).

David is showing that he will hold onto the word, no matter what tempts him away from it, or whatever difficulty he is in (for example, verses 78, 85, 95, 110, 115, 116).

The reason is in v89 "Forever, O LORD, Your word is settled in heaven." God's word is everlasting, and abides in heaven - and that means *with God*. If one takes in the word of God, loves it, meditates on it, does it, then he too will last forever. There is no greater reason to hold onto something than that!

This is largely what the difficult teaching of Jesus is about in the gospel of John. We can be begotten (born again) by the word of God. If we are born of the eternal word, then we too will last forever, and we will be heavenly creations. If we live and breathe the word of God, then we are sons and daughters of His. God wants such to be with Him for eternity. His family. His heritage. His offspring.

Food for thought

Verse 85-86 - There is a powerful exhortation for us in the contrast between the wicked and God's law. We either imitate the wicked or live a life consistent with God's law. The wicked as self seeking – overthrowing others. God's law is faithful – seeking the good of others.

Verse 92 - It was an understanding of the Law of God which helped David to understand his afflictions. Do we use the Bible to measure our daily experiences?

Psalm 119:129-176

Lost and alone inside our consciousness

For days you have trekked through the tunnels and caves inside the mountain. Your supplies are running low. The darkness around you is complete, and you've forgotten what it's like to see the light. Your hands, shoulders and knees are scratched and bleeding because of constant contact with the rock walls and floor you cannot see. Feeling glad of the helmet covering your head, you feel your way, stumbling, onwards.

Can you imagine this? You feel your way round a corner of rock and suddenly become aware that you can see dimly. As you move forward, more and more of the tunnel can be made out - a rough boulder floor, jagged outcrops of rock, but ahead there is light and as you move toward it you suddenly find yourself in a wide open cave, full of light, and full of treasures of gold, silver and precious stones.

If we were to put verse 130 into a story or a scene from a film, maybe it would be a little like that. We live inside our own consciousness, alone and unaware of what each thought and inclination really means. We're stumbling around and feeling our way. We do not know about human nature, what it is, and how to control it. God's word is a light that can enter into our darkness:

The entrance of thy words giveth light; it giveth understanding unto the simple. (Psalm 119:130)

The entrance it's talking about is the entrance to our mind, our psyche, our inner self. The Psalmist also puts it this way:

He shall go to the generation of his fathers; ***they shall never see light****. Man that is in honour, and understandeth not, is like the beasts that perish. (Psalm 49:19-20)*

Without letting the word of God shine inside us, we are just like the animals that have no idea of conscience, morality, or even of self. What a wonderful privilege we have of understanding ourselves. The result of this is explained in verse 133; a path that is not only well lit, but steps that are ordered and going the right direction:

Order my steps in thy word: and let not any iniquity have dominion over me. (Psalm 119:133)

Food for thought

Verse 129 - Because David respected God's words (v129) and realised that they were "righteous and faithful" (v138) he was able to uphold them even in difficult times. The degree to which we are able to maintain our faith is proportionate to how much we value the Scriptures.

Verse 135 - David's desire for the shining face echoes the blessing of Numbers 6:23-27 and Moses' experience when he came down the mount with the tables of the law – Exodus 34:29.

Psalm 120

I am for peace... they are for war

> A Song of degrees. *In my distress I cried unto the LORD, and he heard me. Deliver my soul, O LORD, from lying lips, and from a deceitful tongue. What shall be given unto thee? or what shall be done unto thee, thou false tongue? Sharp arrows of the mighty, with coals of juniper.* **Woe is me, that I sojourn in Mesech, that I dwell in the tents of Kedar!** *My soul hath long dwelt with him that hateth peace. I am for peace: but when I speak, they are for war. (Psalm 120:1-7)*

Joshua 11 tells us about the resistance Israel met when they entered the land of Canaan, from the King of Hazor, King of the Canaanites. Hazor was burned to the ground by Joshua, but when we get to the time of Jeremiah, Hazor is still there, and the people of Kedar dwell there.

Jeremiah 49:28-33 tells us that this is a tent-dwelling people, mostly employed in livestock farming and the keeping and trading of Camels:

> *Concerning Kedar, and concerning the kingdoms of Hazor,*

which Nebuchadrezzar king of Babylon shall smite, thus saith the LORD; Arise ye, go up to Kedar, and spoil the men of the east. Their tents and their flocks shall they take away: they shall take to themselves their curtains, and all their vessels, and their camels; and they shall cry unto them, Fear is on every side. (Jeremiah 49:28-29)

Ezekiel 27:13 tells us that Meshech were a trading nation:

Javan, Tubal, and Meshech, they were thy merchants: they traded the persons of men and vessels of brass in thy market. (Ezekiel 27:13)

Perhaps, at the time the Psalmist is writing Psalm 120, Meshech and Kedar are confederate, using the camels for long trading trips? Perhaps the people of Kedar were descended from Meshech, who was the son of Japheth? In any case, having looked at some background, we're still left with the questions: What did the Psalmist mean? Why was he dwelling with these people? Why were they lying about him? Certainly v7 sounds a lot like the uncomfortable relationship the Jews have always had with the Bedouin people, especially when they returned to Palestine after the First World War.

Food for thought

Verse 5 - Dwelling in the "tents of Kedar" is like the way in which the Song of Solomon speaks of the appearance of the bride – Song 1:5.

Verse 7 - David was amongst those that Jesus described as "blessed" – Matthew 5:9.

Psalm 121

When the sun moved backwards

This Psalm appears to refer to Isaiah 38:8 where God promises to take the shadow of the sun back ten degrees:

> *Behold, I will bring again the shadow of the degrees, which is gone down in the sun dial of Ahaz, ten degrees backward. So the sun returned ten degrees, by which degrees it was gone down. (Isaiah 38:8)*

The title of Psalm 121 is "a song of degrees" and the Psalm mentions a shadow in v5:

> *The LORD is thy keeper: the LORD is thy shade upon thy right hand. (Psalm 121:5)*

Perhaps Hezekiah wrote this as he waited to see if the promise of God would come to pass, and as he checked the sun's shadow on his hand to see if it would advance or retreat?

Food for thought

Verse 1 - In response to his question "from whence cometh my help?" he gives the response (see also Psalm 123:1). He sees the help as coming from God, not the hills where idols are worshipped.

Verse 3-4 - In saying that God "will not slumber" David is expressing a simple truth about God's care for His children – but surprisingly not an expression one finds elsewhere.

Psalm 122

Let us go into the house of the LORD

The heading of the Psalm tells us this is written by David, but when we read the contents it brings up an enigma. In v1-2 he asks:

> A Song of degrees of David. *I was glad when they said unto me, Let us go into the house of the LORD. Our feet shall stand within thy gates, O Jerusalem. (Psalm 122:1-2)*

The problem is, the temple at Jerusalem wasn't built until partway into Solomon's reign, so how can David be talking about going to God's house at Jerusalem? What "house" could David be talking about here?

Food for thought

Verse 4 - In saying "whither the tribes go up" the Psalmist is looking beyond his day to the time of the kingdom, when Israel and Judah will be saved. There was only a short spell during the reign of David when the nation was united in such a way that all the tribes used

Jerusalem as the centre of their worship.

Verse 5 - In saying thrones (plural) the Psalmist is looking to the kingdom when the disciples will sit on 12 thrones (see Matthew 19:28).

Psalm 123

The scorn of those that are at ease

The Psalmist seems to be talking about a time when he, and his fellows were under some kind of subjugation:

> Behold, as the eyes of servants look unto the hand of their masters, and as the eyes of a maiden unto the hand of her mistress; so our eyes wait upon the LORD our God, until that he have mercy upon us. (Psalm 123:2)

What could this be talking about? The heading of the Psalm is "a song of degrees" (see the comment for Psalm 121) so it could be during the time of Hezekiah. The following verse also gives us a clue:

> Our soul is exceedingly filled with the scorning of **those that are at ease**, and with the contempt of the proud. (Psalm 123:4)

The Hebrew word for "those that are at ease" is used only ten times in the Bible, and appears most times in the context of the Sennacherib invasion at the time of Hezekiah:

> *Rise up, ye women **that are at ease**; hear my voice, ye careless daughters; give ear unto my speech. ... Tremble, ye women **that are at ease**; be troubled, ye careless ones: strip you, and make you bare, and gird sackcloth upon your loins. ... And my people shall dwell in a peaceable habitation, and in sure dwellings, **and in quiet** resting places;* (Isaiah 32:9, 11, 18)

Could it be that these wealthy women poured scorn on the young King Hezekiah and his servants?

The word appears again in the prophecy of the judgement of Sennacherib, and this time it is translated "tumult" rather than "quiet":

> *Because thy rage against me, and **thy tumult**, is come up into mine ears, therefore will I put my hook in thy nose, and my bridle in thy lips, and I will turn thee back by the way by which thou camest.* (Isaiah 37:29)

Food for thought

Verse 2 - In the analogies given about the way that servants and maidens look to their masters, we see a beautiful image of how we should regard our God. Both the servant and maiden are required by their master to obey them - not by constraint but willingly - likewise we are to be unstinting in our service (e.g. 1 Peter 5:2).

Verse 3 - One might think that the Psalmist has contempt for himself until we see (v4) that it is others that think so of him. But notice the Psalmist is not seeking to assert his own position. He leaves things in God's hands.

Psalm 124

Passing over the Jordan

Then the waters had overwhelmed us, the stream had gone over our soul: Then the proud waters had gone over our soul. (Psalm 124:4-5)

David is likening the situation of Israel and its enemies to crossing a stream of water, where God had saved them from being covered over by that water. He is reminding them of how God saved them at the time of Joshua, where they entered the land of Canaan by crossing the Jordan. See the similar language to this Psalm in Joshua:

*That **the waters** which came down from above **stood and rose up** upon an heap very far from the city Adam, that is beside Zaretan: and those that came down toward the sea of the plain, even the salt sea, failed, and were cut off: and **the people passed over** right against Jericho. (Joshua 3:16)*

*For the LORD your God dried up the waters of Jordan from before you, until **ye were passed over**, as the LORD your God did to the Red sea, which he dried up from before us, until **we***

were gone over. *(Joshua 4:23)*

But why would David be thinking of this historical event now? The answer may be that he had just experienced the same journey over the Jordan, and this time it was his own people that threatened to overwhelm him (see 2Sam 17 and especially v20-22):

> *And it came to pass, after they were departed, that they came up out of the well, and went and told king David, and said unto David, Arise, and* **pass quickly over the water:** *for thus hath Ahithophel counselled against you. Then David arose, and all the people that were with him, and* **they passed over Jordan:** *by the morning light there lacked not one of them that was not* **gone over** *Jordan. (2 Samuel 17:21-22)*

Food for thought

Verse 1-3 - The Psalmist - against the background of severe trial of an enemy - sees exactly who had given deliverance. It is so easy to seek God when in difficulty but to forget Him when the problem is over.

Verse 8 - Notice that God is the creator and it is the creator who helps. We cannot view an acceptance that God created the heavens and the earth as an optional belief. It is integral to a belief that God works to save His children. He can save *because* He is the creator.

Psalm 125

Mount Zion cannot be moved

> A Song of degrees. *They that trust in the LORD shall be as mount Zion, which cannot be removed, but abideth for ever. (Psalm 125:1)*

The symbol of "Zion, which cannot be removed" is explained in Hebrews, and contrasted with another mountain which shook:

> *But ye are come unto* **mount Sion**, *and unto the city of the living God, the heavenly Jerusalem, and to an innumerable company of angels, To the general assembly and church of the firstborn, which are written in heaven, and to God the Judge of all, and to the spirits of just men made perfect, And to Jesus the mediator of the new covenant, and to the blood of sprinkling, that speaketh better things than that of Abel. See that ye refuse not him that speaketh. For if they escaped not who refused him that spake on earth, much more shall not we escape, if we turn away from him that speaketh from heaven:* **Whose voice then shook the earth**: *but now he hath promised, saying,*

*Yet **once more I shake not the earth only**, but also heaven. And this word, Yet once more, signifieth the removing of those things that are **shaken**, as of things that are made, that **those things which cannot be shaken may remain**. Wherefore we receiving a kingdom which **cannot be moved**, let us have grace, whereby we may serve God acceptably with reverence and godly fear: For our God is a consuming fire. (Hebrews 12:22-29).*

So Sinai is the analogy of the Old Covenant, which could be shaken, as mount Sinai shook when Moses received the law. Zion is the analogy of the New Covenant, which cannot be removed, as it says in our Psalm.

So the New Testament gospel is rooted in the Old Testament.

Food for thought

Verse 3 - In speaking of the way that the righteous will be delivered from the wicked, God recognises that the wicked can influence the righteous to do evil.

Verse 5 - Whilst the Psalm might appear to be talking about the land of Israel and the city of Zion, the way in which Paul (Galatians 6:16) quotes this verse shows that the Psalm is speaking of the faithful servants of God, not just a physical land and city.

Psalm 126

The captivity of Zion

> A Song of degrees. *When the LORD turned again the captivity of Zion, we were like them that dream.* (Psalm 126:1)

The captivity of Zion (v1) is also mentioned in Psalm 137:

> *By the rivers of Babylon, there we sat down, yea, we wept, when we remembered Zion. ... For there they that carried us away captive required of us a song; and they that wasted us required of us mirth, saying, Sing us one of the songs of Zion.* (Psalm 137:1, 3)

If these two Psalms are related, then Psalm 126 must have been written some time during the captivity in Babylon, which happened in stages as described in 2 Chronicles 36.

The gladness in verse 2 seems to suggest that this captivity has been ended, at least partially:

> *Then was our mouth filled with laughter, and our tongue with singing: then said they among the heathen, The LORD hath*

done great things for them. (Psalm 126:2)

Perhaps it is referring to the time during the reign of King Cyrus, when they were allowed to go back to Jerusalem?

> *Now in the first year of Cyrus king of Persia, that the word of the LORD spoken by the mouth of Jeremiah might be accomplished, the LORD stirred up the spirit of Cyrus king of Persia, that he made a proclamation throughout all his kingdom, and put it also in writing, saying, Thus saith Cyrus king of Persia, All the kingdoms of the earth hath the LORD God of heaven given me; and he hath charged me to build him an house in Jerusalem, which is in Judah. Who is there among you of all his people? The LORD his God be with him, and let him go up. (2 Chronicles 36:22-23)*

Food for thought

Verse 2 - Notice it is the heathen (non Jews) who recognise God's goodness towards those who trust in Him.

Verse 4 - The Psalmist likens their return to the "streams in the South" because in the desert in summer the streams dry up and only reappear in the spring after the rain. A dry and barren land comes to life after the rain even though it looks, humanly speaking, as if it is totally barren. So it was with the regathering of Israel in the 1900s. The world did not expect it. However it was prophecied to happen with the same degree of certainty as rain causing dried up streams to come to life again.

Psalm 127

Men whose teeth are spears and arrows

> *As arrows are in the hand of a mighty man; so are children of the youth. Happy is the man that hath his quiver full of them: they shall not be ashamed, but they shall speak with the enemies in the gate. (Psalm 127:4-5)*

In talking about children as sharp arrows, David may be thinking of the example of Joab, Abishai and Asahel, the three sons of Zeruiah. All three of these brothers were formidable fighting men, and instrumental in setting David up as King.

David uses this same idea of arrows to describe the men he was with in the cave when he fled from Saul, and on this occasion this could also have been describing the three sons of Zeruiah:

> *My soul is among lions: and I lie even among them that are set on fire, even the sons of men, **whose teeth are spears and arrows**, and their tongue a sharp sword. (Psalm 57:4)*

Food for thought

Verse 1 - Ezra understood that when God was watching over His people there was no need for an armed guard – Ezra 8:22.

Verse 3 - The linking of children (v3) and the Lord building the house (v1) shows that this Psalm is a comment on the promise of 2 Samuel 7:8-17. Whilst David wanted to build God a house He told David that He would build David a house - this house was to be a house of people. We, if we believe and are baptised, are part of this house of David.

Psalm 128

Does God really bless those who walk in His ways?

> *A Song of degrees. Blessed is every one that feareth the LORD; that walketh in his ways. For thou shalt eat the labour of thine hands:* **happy shalt thou be**, *and it shall be well with thee.* (Psalm 128:1-2)

Nearly two decades ago when I first wrote about this Psalm, I questioned where the blessings promised in the Psalm were there for me. I had no wife, no children, and my life was more or less a mess.

At this point I could have concluded one of two things:

1) God isn't true to His promises. He should be blessing me, and hasn't. Or,

2) God is always true to His promises. He hasn't blessed me yet. Perhaps I need to change my attitude, and He will bless me in good time?

The first attitude is easy to adopt because it blames someone else. It's the broad path that many take, and ultimately leads to rejecting God.

The second attitude is difficult to adopt because it blames ourselves and asks us to change and to put in the hard work of building. It's the narrow path that few take, but ultimately leads to the blessings promised by God.

None of us can be described as "walking in His ways" right away. All of us need work. The Psalm talks about building a house - and that doesn't happen overnight! In the same way, blessings also take time to come to us, and they surely will! Just as you can't enjoy the house while building it, until the hard, consistent labour has been done, so it is in our own lives. The fruits of righteousness, walking in wisdom, and trusting in God, will come with time.

If in doubt, the Bible provides plenty of examples of this. For example, look at David who made many mistakes along the way, yet this could be said of him at the end:

> *And he died in a good old age, full of days, riches, and honour: and Solomon his son reigned in his stead. (1Ch 29:28)*

Food for thought

Verse 3 - In speaking of "thy wife" as a "fruitful vine" (v3), the Psalmist sees the faithful wife as a cameo of how the nation should be. Israel had been, at one time, a fruitful vine (Ezekiel 19:10).

Verse 5-6 - The blessing out of Zion and peace upon Israel will be seen in the kingdom, when Christ returns to sit on the throne of David.

Psalm 129

The youth of the nation of Israel

> *A Song of degrees.* Many a time have they afflicted me from my youth, may Israel now say: Many a time have they afflicted me from my youth: yet they have not prevailed against me. *(Psalm 129:1-2)*

The period when Israel was first a nation is recorded in the book of Judges. So, in verses 1-2 the Psalmist is probably referring to the history of Israel at the time of the Judges. In verse 4 we have a phrase that reminds us of one of the judges:

> *The LORD is righteous: he hath cut asunder the cords of the wicked. (Psalm 129:4)*

The bonds being cut is figurative, but this did literally happen at the time of Samson:

> *And when he came unto Lehi, the Philistines shouted against him: and the Spirit of the LORD came mightily upon him, and the cords that were upon his arms became as flax that was burnt*

with fire, and his bands loosed from off his hands. (Judges 15:14)

Food for thought

Verse 3 - "the plowers plowed upon my back" is taken up in Micah 3:12 to speak of judgement that was to come. This was spoken to Hezekiah (Jeremiah 26:18). Whilst King Hezekiah listened to the prophet, Israel generally did not - hence the comment by the Psalmist.

Verse 5 - Jerusalem was repeatedly overthrown because of the faithlessness of Israel. However the true servant of God will continue to pray (verse 5) that Jerusalem's enemies will be confounded because Jerusalem's enemies are God's enemies. This is what it is to "pray for the peace of Jerusalem" Psalm 122:6 and "mourn" Matthew 5:4.

Psalm 130

God does not keep hold of our sins

In the Garden of Eden, God put Adam there to tend and **keep** it. When he and his wife sinned, God put Cherubim in front of the entrance to the garden to **keep** the way to the tree of life. When Cain slew Abel, his reply to God's questioning was "am I my brother's **keeper**?" And when God revealed His plan of salvation to Abraham He said "Thou shalt **keep** my covenant therefore, thou, and thy seed after thee in their generations."

Tracing this word through its first four occurrences in the Bible gives us a potted history of mankind. Adam should have **kept** the garden rather than bothering with the tree of good and evil. Through sin God had to **keep** him away from the tree of life. By not **keeping** his brother Abel safe, Cain did evil and was cast away from his family. By **keeping** God's covenant mankind could find a way back to God.

In verses 3-4 the Psalmist says:

> If thou, LORD, shouldest **mark** (Hebrew "keep") iniquities, O Lord, who shall stand? But there is forgiveness with thee, that thou mayest be feared. (Psalm 130:3-4)

In using the same Hebrew word for "keep", is he referring back to those early days in the plan of God with mankind? Is David pulling out the main lesson for us from those early chapters of Genesis? God does not **keep** hold of our sins — He casts them away if we ask Him.

Food for thought

Verse 4 - Seems paradoxical doesn't it? That God should be feared because He forgives sins. One might have thought He would be feared if he did not forgive our sins. The "fear" here is not terror, it is respect - for if He didn't forgive (v3) then we would not stand.

Verse 6 - The way that the Psalmist speaks about waiting for God should be how we are in our expectation of the return of Jesus. We should be like the watchman after a long night watch, longing for the morning light to arrive.

Psalm 131

Lifted up in pride

> A Song of degrees of David. *LORD, my heart is not haughty, nor mine eyes lofty: neither do I exercise myself in great matters, or in things too high for me. (Psalm 131:1)*

What does David mean when he says "my heart is not haughty?" The English word "haughty", translated from the Hebrew word "gabahh", has its first occurrence in the Bible in 1 Samuel 10:23, and that's no accident. Here we read about Saul, the newly chosen King:

> *And they ran and fetched him thence: and when he stood among the people, he was higher (gabahh) than any of the people from his shoulders and upward. (1 Samuel 10:23)*

David is saying that he will not make the same mistakes that Saul did in lifting himself up, in pride, above the people. David will remain a humble servant.

In comparison with Saul, another King called Jehoshaphat was "lifted up", but notice what he was lifted up in:

*And his heart was **lifted up in the ways of the LORD**: moreover he took away the high places and groves out of Judah. (2 Chronicles 17:6)*

What about us? Do we lift ourselves up in pride, or are we lifted up by the ways of the LORD?

Food for thought

Psalm - David provides a powerful warning about trying to understand things beyond what is revealed. It is so easy to speculate or worry about things which we are not told. So many of the arguments we have can stem from speculation, using non Biblical language, about things we are not told. David says that the "weaned child" mentality that he had should be ours.

Verse 2 - If we view ourselves as mature, no longer babies, we will desire the "'meat" mentioned in Hebrews 5:14. Indeed if we think that we still need the milk we have to view ourselves as "unskilful" (Hebrews 5:13) and not yet weaned. So seeing ourselves as needing milk is not a sign of humility. If we need milk we are immature.

Psalm 132

David's vow: to house the Ark of the Covenant

Clearly at an early age David became concerned that the God of Israel was dwelling in a tent. We can gather this because of his mention of his own tent:

> *Surely I will not come into the tabernacle of my house, nor go up into my bed. (Psalm 132:3)*

While in contrast he realised the Ark wasn't in a house:

> *We will go into his tabernacles: we will worship at his footstool. Arise, O LORD, into thy rest; thou, and the ark of thy strength. (Psalm 132:7-8)*

So he made a vow:

> *How he sware unto the LORD, and vowed unto the mighty God of Jacob; Surely I will not come into the tabernacle of my house, nor go up into my bed; I will not give sleep to mine eyes, or slumber to mine eyelids, Until I find out a place for the LORD,*

an habitation for the mighty God of Jacob. (Psalm 132:2-5)

Later in his life, he states his wish to resolve this issue more definitely, referring to his desire to build the temple:

That the king said unto Nathan the prophet, see now, I dwell in an house of cedar, but the ark of God dwelleth within curtains. (2 Samuel 7:2)

Food for thought

Verse 2 - The "mighty God of Jacob" is the God of the blessings (Genesis 49:24).

Verse 6 - This Psalm shows that David was thinking about the resting place for the Ark whilst he was a shepherd boy in Bethlehem. "Ephratah" (v6) is Bethlehem (Micah 5:2). David left Bethlehem around the time he killed Goliath - as a young man. So we see that David's desire to put the ark in Zion was not something that he thought up when he was king. Rather it was the driving force in all his life. Maybe this is why he is called "a man after [God's] own heart" (Acts 13:22).

Psalm 133

The blessing of life for evermore

In verse 2 and 3 of this Psalm, David is considering the dew of God that runs down the mountains of Israel and brings life to the people of Israel every morning. He likens it to the anointing of the High Priest:

> *It is like the precious ointment upon the head, that ran down upon the beard, even Aaron's beard: that went down to the skirts of his garments; As the dew of Hermon, and as the dew that descended upon the mountains of Zion: for there the LORD commanded the blessing, even life for evermore. (Psalm 133:2-3)*

When Aaron was anointed, the oil was poured onto a plate (the crown) tied to his mitre which had engraved on it "Holiness to the LORD":

> *And thou shalt make a plate of pure gold, and grave upon it, like the engravings of a signet, HOLINESS TO THE LORD. And thou shalt put it on a blue lace, that it may be upon the mitre; upon the forefront of the mitre it shall be. (Exodus 28:36-37)*

Holy means "set apart". Perhaps David is drawing the comparison to say that all people of the land can be equally special to God no matter where in it they lived - whether Hermon to the far North or Zion to the South? He is also making the point that while the source of the river Jordan is Mount Hermon, the source of salvation is from Zion.

Food for thought

Verse 1 - Unity is such an important issue that it forms the first thing that Paul speaks of when describing a living sacrifice (see Romans 12). Also amongst all the problems the Corinthian brethren had, it was the first thing he addressed there too (see 1 Corinthians 3).

Verse 3 - The promise that God will show the blessing which He has commanded shows the fulfilment of Leviticus 25:21 where the release of slaves prefigures the redemption from sin and death.

Psalm 134

In the house of the LORD by night

A Song of degrees. Behold, bless ye the LORD, all ye servants of the LORD, which by night stand in the house of the LORD. (Psalm 134:1)

It seems like an odd phrase in verse 1. What does it mean to stand in the house of the LORD? Who would go into the house of the LORD at night, when the doors would be shut and guarded? Could this be talking about the Priest, who needed to keep the lamp burning through the night?

Without the vail of the testimony, in the tabernacle of the congregation, shall Aaron order it from the evening unto the morning before the LORD continually: it shall be a statute for ever in your generations. (Leviticus 24:3)

But the Psalm seems to speak to many people, not just the few. There was only one other function that could be performed in the temple at night, but we don't find it stipulated in the Law. We find the answer in the words of Solomon:

> *That thine eyes may be open toward this house night and day, even toward the place of which thou hast said, My name shall be there: that thou mayest hearken unto the prayer which thy servant shall make toward this place. (1 Kings 8:29)*

And the words of Nehemiah:

> *Let thine ear now be attentive, and thine eyes open, that thou mayest hear the prayer of thy servant, which I pray before thee now, day and night, for the children of Israel thy servants, and confess the sins of the children of Israel, which we have sinned against thee: both I and my father's house have sinned. (Nehemiah 1:6)*

These both mention prayer in relation to the temple at night. So the Psalmist is saying that by prayer to God, we may stand in His house, wherever we are, and whatever time it is, day or night. It is those who pray by (or on) their beds that are described as being in the sanctuary of God in verse 2. This is comforting for us Gentiles, because we have no other temple to go to:

> *Lift up your hands in the sanctuary, and bless the LORD. (Psalm 134:2)*

Food for thought

Verse 3 - The Lord who has created the universe is quite capable of providing blessings to His servants. A certain belief in creation provides the confidence to believe that God will work in our lives too.

Verse 3 - In speaking of the blessing out of Zion, the Psalmist is echoing the ideas of Psalm 133, which has fellowship as the basis for the blessing being given.

Psalm 135

For I know that the LORD is great

This Psalm shows how God's name became associated with the great salvation He achieved for the people of Israel:

> *For I know that the LORD is great, and that our Lord is above all gods ... Who smote the firstborn of Egypt, both of man and beast. Who sent tokens and wonders into the midst of thee, O Egypt, upon Pharaoh, and upon all his servants. (Psalm 135:5, 8-9)*

It explains that the plagues happened so that in hearing of His great works, the Gentile people might seek to serve Him too. In the days before social media, TV, the internet, radio or newspapers, the fame of God's name still needed to spread somehow through word of mouth, and it was these great events that made that happen:

> *Thy name, O LORD, endureth for ever; and thy memorial, O LORD, throughout all generations. (Psalm 135:13)*

This is not just an idea confined to the Psalm. In the Exodus account

God Himself says to Moses why He is causing the plagues to happen:

> *And I will harden Pharaoh's heart, that he shall follow after them; and I will be honoured upon Pharaoh, and upon all his host; that the Egyptians may know that I am the LORD. And they did so. (Exodus 14:4)*

Food for thought

Verse 4 - In speaking of Israel as a "peculiar treasure" the Psalmist is echoing the description of the nation (see Exodus 19:5) where the same, rare, Hebrew word is used. Likewise we can be a "peculiar people" (1 Peter 2:9) with the same calling as the nation of Israel.

Verse 8-12 - In re-stating what happened in Egypt, the Psalmist is rehearsing a very powerful reminder. In remembering what God had done in the past he is reinforcing his conviction that his God is at work in his own life. Maybe we should do the same - reflect on the way that we know that God has worked to encourage us about the future?

Psalm 136

O give thanks to the LORD, for His mercy endureth forever

It is clear from the first three verses that this Psalm is about giving thanks to God:

> O give thanks unto the LORD; for he is good: for his mercy endureth for ever. O give thanks unto the God of gods: for his mercy endureth for ever. O give thanks to the Lord of lords: for his mercy endureth for ever. (Psalm 136:1-3)

There follows a list of twenty things to give thanks for, finishing off in verse 26 with a repeat of the call to give thanks.

Now then; if I were to make a list of twenty things to thank God for, what would I put in that list? I wouldn't have thought of many of the things in this Psalm, that's for sure. And what order would I put them in? I think giving thanks for food would be near the top of my list but where does it come in this list? In fact, does the writer of the Psalm list anything that is completely personal to him?

What are we being taught by this Psalm? Perhaps that God wants us to understand His work deeply and to praise Him for those things that are truly His handiwork. Yes, we might also thank Him for the things that from our own self absorbed perspective seem important, but we should also take the time to understand His great works throughout history and thank Him for those things that happened long ago or that happen outside our immediate daily experience.

Food for thought

Verse 5 - That God made the heavens by "wisdom" or "understanding" is echoed in Proverbs 3:19. Also Job 39:26 implies that God makes the hawk fly by His wisdom. That same wisdom of God also conceived the plan of salvation through faith in the risen Jesus. If we, in our foolishness, think that the universe came into existence by accident, then what do we think about the wisdom of salvation through Christ? Or is that, like it was to the Greeks, foolishness to us? (1 Corinthians 1:18).

Verse 11 - In speaking of Israel being brought "from among them" speaking of the deliverance of Israel from Egypt, the Psalmist is highlighting that Israel were not simply removed from the land but that they were separated from them – a matter of fellowship. Sadly Israel, whilst in Egypt, had started to imitate the Egyptians rather than remain a separate Godly nation.

Psalm 137

Edom's hatred of Jerusalem

It appears from verse 7 of this Psalm that the Edomites had a hand in the destruction of Jerusalem at the time of the Babylon invasion:

Remember, O LORD, the children of Edom in the day of Jerusalem; who said, Rase it, rase it, even to the foundation thereof. (Psalm 137:7)

It is also evident from 2 Chronicles 36:17-19 that this destruction was complete:

Therefore he brought upon them the king of the Chaldees, who slew their young men with the sword in the house of their sanctuary, and had no compassion upon young man or maiden, old man, or him that stooped for age: he gave them all into his hand. And all the vessels of the house of God, great and small, and the treasures of the house of the LORD, and the treasures of the king, and of his princes; all these he brought to Babylon. And they burnt the house of God, and brake down the wall of Jerusalem, and burnt all the palaces thereof with fire, and destroyed all the goodly vessels thereof. (2 Chronicles 36:17-19)

The Psalm appears to suggest that, had it not been for the Edomites, that destruction would have been less severe. God's judgment on Edom would therefore also be severe, as we can see in Isaiah 34:

For my sword shall be bathed in heaven: behold, it shall come down upon Idumea, and upon the people of my curse, to judgment. ... For it is the day of the LORD'S vengeance, and the year of recompences for the controversy of Zion. (Isaiah 34:5, 8)

Food for thought

Verse 5 - In desiring not to forget Jerusalem, the Psalmist is showing us where his heart is. Of course he is not thinking simply of a physical location but rather of all the things of God which are tied into the place. It is for this reason that Solomon anticipated that men would pray towards Jerusalem (1 Kings 8:30, 35) and why Daniel disregarded the king's command (Daniel 6:10).

Verse 7 - The call to "remember Edom" is reflected in the prophecy of Obadiah (see verse 12).

Psalm 138

A matter of perspective

Notice the comparison between the following two verses from this Psalm and the next:

> *Though the LORD be high, yet hath he respect unto the lowly: but **the proud he knoweth afar off**. (Psalm 138:6)*

> *Thou knowest my downsitting and mine uprising, **thou understandest my thought afar off**. (Psalm 139:2)*

God knows the actions of every one of us, even from a long way away. For some that is positive, and for others it is negative. It all depends on our point of view.

Food for thought

Verse 2 - If God has magnified His word above His name, how much do we value it? Is it something we can take or leave at will? Is it something that we read with love and joy, or do we try to make its message fit our own preferences?

Verse 6 - If God can humble Himself to "behold the things ... in the earth" (see also Psalm 113:6-7), we should have no problems "condescending to men of low degree" (Rom 12:16).

Psalm 139

Thine eyes did see my substance

I t is one thing to understand that God knows all our thoughts and sees all our actions (v1-6) but it is quite another thing to actually invite it:

> To the chief Musician, A Psalm of David. *O LORD, thou hast searched me, and known me. Thou knowest my downsitting and mine uprising, thou understandest my thought afar off. Thou compassest my path and my lying down, and art acquainted with all my ways. For there is not a word in my tongue, but, lo, O LORD, thou knowest it altogether. Thou hast beset me behind and before, and laid thine hand upon me. Such knowledge is too wonderful for me; it is high, I cannot attain unto it. (Psalm 139:1-6)*

David goes on to ask God to search his heart. In our prayers, do we invite this kind of scrutiny?

> *Search me, O God, and know my heart: try me, and know my thoughts: And see if there be any wicked way in me, and lead*

me in the way everlasting. (Psalm 139:23-24)

Part of the reason is that David realises he can't get away from God anyway:

Whither shall I go from thy spirit? or whither shall I flee from thy presence? If I ascend up into heaven, thou art there: if I make my bed in hell, behold, thou art there. If I take the wings of the morning, and dwell in the uttermost parts of the sea; Even there shall thy hand lead me, and thy right hand shall hold me. If I say, Surely the darkness shall cover me; even the night shall be light about me. Yea, the darkness hideth not from thee; but the night shineth as the day: the darkness and the light are both alike to thee. (Psalm 139:7-12)

And he realises that when he was helpless and, as yet, unformed in the womb, it was a good thing that God could see him!

For thou hast possessed my reins: thou hast covered me in my mother's womb. I will praise thee; for I am fearfully and wonderfully made: marvellous are thy works; and that my soul knoweth right well. My substance was not hid from thee, when I was made in secret, and curiously wrought in the lowest parts of the earth. ***Thine eyes did see my substance****, yet being unperfect; and in thy book all my members were written, which in continuance were fashioned, when as yet there was none of them. (Psalm 139:13-16)*

He concludes that the fact that God knows all, is rather a good thing for him:

> *How precious also are thy thoughts unto me, O God! how great is the sum of them! (Psalm 139:17)*

Just as in the womb it was only God who could see us and look after us, so in death it is only God who can remember what we were and bring our substance back from decay. Jonah sought to run away from God, finding himself at last in a more perfect and complete hiding place than anyone could deem possible — the belly of a fish, deep in the sea. It was a good thing for Jonah that God could still see him and hear his prayer! Should we not likewise rejoice in God's knowledge of us in our waking lives? It may feel uncomfortable that He knows and sees everything, but ultimately it is that trait that saves us.

Food for thought

Verse 22 - We often have ill feelings towards others. However we do well to reflect on the way that David dealt, in his mind, with such people. His hatred was "perfect" – that is in a way consistent with the way that God feels and reacts to those that oppose Him.

Verse 23 - Interestingly the call for God to "search" the Psalmist is echoed by Jeremiah (17:10) after saying that the heart is deceitful. It is just because we are deceitful that we should want God to search our hearts, for we cannot trust our own judgement.

Psalm 140

How to act towards people who hate you

Do you know people that hate you? I mean *really* hate you? David did. David had "friends" who wanted him dead. How awful it must have been to be in the presence of those people when he knew their smooth words were a mask for their hatred?

The answer David gives to the problem is to do nothing, and then to pray, because God would maintain his cause:

> *I know that the LORD will maintain the cause of the afflicted, and the right of the poor. (Psalm 140:12)*

At the same time he trusted that God would cause justice to be served:

> *Let burning coals fall upon them: let them be cast into the fire; into deep pits, that they rise not up again. (Psalm 140:10)*

The writer in Proverbs further explains the concept of burning coals like this:

If thine enemy be hungry, give him bread to eat; and if he be thirsty, give him water to drink: For thou shalt heap coals of fire upon his head, and the LORD shall reward thee. (Proverbs 25:21-22)

So if someone hates you, be courteous to them, because God is the judge of all men, and if He sees you acting this way but nevertheless afflicted by the wicked, He will act to "maintain the cause of the afflicted."

Food for thought

Verse 3 - "The poison of asps is under their lips" is quoted in Romans 3:13 and contrasts with Song of Solomon 4:11, where the bride's lips drop as an honeycomb. We have to decide whether we have poison or the honeycomb at our lips. We cannot have both.

Verse 3-4 - The evil man of this Psalm is not simply someone who happens to do evil things. He is one who plans evil and sets about achieving evil ends. In sharpening his tongue (v3) he calculates what to say. This is why the Psalmist says (v4) he "purposed" to do evil.

Psalm 141

Trusting in God when depressed

> *Our bones are scattered at the grave's mouth, as when one cutteth and cleaveth wood upon the earth. (Psalm 141:7)*

If we take this Psalm as being written at the same time as Psalm 140 and 141 (see comment for Psalm 142), then David and his men are hiding in caves:

> Maschil of David; A Prayer when he was in the cave. *I cried unto the LORD with my voice; with my voice unto the LORD did I make my supplication. (Psalm 142:1)*

The same word for "cave" in the heading to Psalm 142 is used of graves, since in Israel caves were used as burial sites. Presumably David was at this time quite depressed and visualizing the woodcuttings at the mouth of the cave he is hiding in, as if they were his bones and the bones of his men. His conclusion in verses 8-10 is an example to us all, in that he banishes such thoughts by trusting in God, the one who can deliver us from all our troubles:

But mine eyes are unto thee, O GOD the Lord: in thee is my trust; leave not my soul destitute. Keep me from the snares which they have laid for me, and the gins of the workers of iniquity. Let the wicked fall into their own nets, whilst that I withal escape. (Psalm 141:8-10)

Food for thought

Verse 3 - the idea of keeping the door of our lips speaks to us about the importance of the way in which we speak. Solomon also says similar things (Ecclesiastes 5:2). The tongue is a little member (James 3:5) yet it can get us into a terrible amount of trouble!

Verse 5 - The effect of the rebuke of the "righteous" is interesting. It is seen by David as being like an anointing! How do we respond to the faithful rebuke of our fellow believers?

Psalm 142

Deliver me from my persecutors, for they are stronger than I

The context of this Psalm is the same as that of the previous two. All three Psalms speak of snares and traps being laid secretly for David, so it appears that the three are linked. The heading of this Psalm tells us that it was written while David was in the cave, so we could assume that all three Psalms are about the time when David fled from Saul and took refuge in the cave of Adullam (1Sam 22):

> *Attend unto my cry; for I am brought very low: deliver me from my persecutors; for they are stronger than I. (Psalm 142:6)*

David was well aware that Saul and his army were stronger than he. This must have weighed heavy on him, since there were men, women and children with him. He would have felt the burden of their well-being on his own shoulders.

So David placed his burden upon the Lord, allowing Him to take on the responsibility for his life and the life of those with him:

> ...I cried unto the LORD with my voice; with my voice unto the LORD did I make my supplication. I poured out my complaint before him; I shewed before him my trouble. (Psalm 142:1-2)

It is important for us, too, to realise that the difficulties we face in life are bigger and stronger than us, and in doing so, to allow God to take them on for us. This is how true peace of mind can be developed:

> Wherefore, if God so clothe the grass of the field, which to day is, and to morrow is cast into the oven, shall he not much more clothe you, O ye of little faith? Therefore take no thought, saying, What shall we eat? or, What shall we drink? or, Wherewithal shall we be clothed? ... for your heavenly Father knoweth that ye have need of all these things. But seek ye first the kingdom of God, and his righteousness; and all these things shall be added unto you. (Matthew 6:30-33)

Food for thought

Note - The title of this Psalm tells us that it was written by David when he was fleeing from Saul. Despite being fearful of Saul and anxious about his future, David took time out to instruct others - 1 Samuel 22:1-2 and Psalm 34:11-22 (this Psalm was written at this time - see the title).

Verse 2-3 - There is no holding back here. David "poured out his complaint" – rather like the Psalmist in the title of Psalm 102. Do we feel able to speak so frankly to our God?

Psalm 143

Being justified (made righteous)

David is obviously in mortal danger while he prays the prayer recorded in Psalm 143. It is a desperate plea to God for help. The interesting thing about it is in verse 2:

> *And enter not into judgment with thy servant:* **for in thy sight shall no man living be justified.** *(Psalm 143:2)*

Notice that he mentions that no-one is justified - and the word "justified" means "righteous" or "sinless". It suggests the reason David was in trouble, was because God was chastening him for his sin. This fits in with the time period after his sin with Bathsheba (see 2 Samuel 12). David's plea isn't merely for God to save him from trouble, but from the cause of that trouble; namely his own sin. In v6-7 we see how desperately he longed for that forgiveness:

> *I stretch forth my hands unto thee: my soul thirsteth after thee, as a thirsty land. Selah. Hear me speedily, O LORD: my spirit faileth: hide not thy face from me, lest I be like unto them that go down into the pit. (Psalm 143:6-7)*

The lesson for us is in v11-12 - note the phrase "for your righteousness sake":

> Quicken me, O LORD, **for thy name's sake: for thy righteousness' sake** bring my soul out of trouble. And **of thy mercy** cut off mine enemies, and destroy all them that afflict my soul: for I am thy servant. (Psalm 143:11-12)

So David had come to realise that there was no self justification for his sin. The only option open to him was to appeal to God's righteousness and His mercy. The same goes for us:

> Therefore by the deeds of the law there shall no flesh be justified in his sight: for by the law is the knowledge of sin. ... For all have sinned, and come short of the glory of God; **Being justified freely by his grace** through the redemption that is in Christ Jesus: (Romans 3:20, 23-24)

God had provided His son to declare God's righteousness, so that, as David understood, justification might be seen by all to result from God's goodness, grace and mercy:

> Whom God hath set forth to be a propitiation through faith in his blood, to declare his righteousness for the remission of sins that are past, through the forbearance of God; To declare, I say, at this time his righteousness: that he might be just, and the justifier of him which believeth in Jesus. (Romans 3:25-26)

Food for thought

Verse 3-4 - We should not underestimate the impact of those who opposed David on his life and his spirituality. Further, we should realise that the way we speak of our fellow believers will impact on the way in which they serve God. If we are negative it will be unhelpful. If we are positive it will help to build them up.

Verse 6 - We saw the lifting up of hands in Psalm 88:9 and 141:2, and we also are encouraged to "pray lifting up holy hands" in 1 Timothy 2:8.

Psalm 144

The LORD my Rock

Notice the language David uses to describe God, and consider that he might have been taking refuge in the rock caves of En-Gedi at the time:

> A Psalm of David. *Blessed be the LORD **my Rock**, Who trains my hands for war, And my fingers for battle— My lovingkindness and **my fortress**, My **high tower** and my deliverer, My shield and **the One in whom I take refuge**, Who subdues my people under me. (Psalm 144:1-2 NKJV)*

At this time it may literally have felt that God was their only hope, the rock within which they were taking refuge. It was here that men gathered to David, many of whom had their own problems, so that David saw it as a miracle that these men were willingly subject to him as their leader:

> *And every one that was in distress, and every one that was in debt, and every one that was discontented, gathered themselves unto him; and he became a captain over them: and there were*

with him about four hundred men. (1 Samuel 22:2)

David may have been thinking about Moses who had a similar problem, stuck in the wilderness with argumentative and dissatisfied people. The word "rock" (Hebrew tsuwr) that David uses for God is first used in the book of Exodus:

Behold, I will stand before thee there upon the rock in Horeb; and thou shalt smite the rock, and there shall come water out of it, that the people may drink. And Moses did so in the sight of the elders of Israel. (Exodus 17:6)

And the LORD said, Behold, there is a place by me, and thou shalt stand upon a rock: And it shall come to pass, while my glory passeth by, that I will put thee in a clift of the rock, and will cover thee with my hand while I pass by: (Exodus 33:21-22)

It was when Moses brought water out of the rock that the people were quieted (Deut 8:15), and in Deuteronomy 32, the Song of Moses, the whole song establishes God as the Rock:

*Because I will publish the name of the LORD: ascribe ye greatness unto **our God. He is the Rock**, his work is perfect: for all his ways are judgment: a God of truth and without iniquity, just and right is he. (Deuteronomy 32:3-4)*

Food for thought

Verse 1 - It might seem incongruous to see a servant blessing God for the ability to fight. However David fought the Lord's battles and so his praise of God is most appropriate. The commandment to drive out the wicked inhabitants of the land had come straight from God (see for example Exodus 23:23-24).

Verse 4, 8 - Man is "vanity" so, if he is not careful, all he speaks is also "vanity".

Psalm 145

Proclaim God's goodness

We're probably used to the idea of preaching. It tends to involve spreading the message of the gospel of salvation. But in this Psalm, which is about spreading the news about God, how much of it involves the message of salvation?

For example, in v4 David declares God's "mighty acts":

> *One generation shall praise thy works to another, and shall declare thy mighty acts. (Psalm 145:4)*

In verse 7, it is His great goodness and righteousness:

> *They shall abundantly utter the memory of thy great goodness, and shall sing of thy righteousness. (Psalm 145:7)*

In verse 9, it is that He is good to all:

> *The LORD is good to all: and his tender mercies are over all his works. (Psalm 145:9)*

It seems to me that the Psalm is suggesting we talk to others about God's character and His achievements. For example, it might involve speaking about how God has saved us from some trouble or anxiety (v14,19):

> *The LORD upholdeth all that fall, and raiseth up all those that be bowed down ... He will fulfil the desire of them that fear him: he also will hear their cry, and will save them. (Psalm 145:14, 19)*

Or how He answered our prayer for something we needed (v15-16):

> *The eyes of all wait upon thee; and thou givest them their meat in due season. Thou openest thine hand, and satisfiest the desire of every living thing. (Psalm 145:15-16)*

Notice that the Psalmist is not necessarily talking about what he will say to unbelievers. How regularly do we talk to our families and friends, even those who already believe in God, about who He is and the things He has done? What else can we find in this chapter worth talking to others about?

Food for thought

Verse 4 - Praise is not something which only gives glory to God. It is a process of educating others also. In telling the following generations of the goodness of God we are praising Him. If we can speak of the way in which God has worked in our lives then those following on after us will find it easier to have the same confidence.

Verse 8 - One of the many places in Scripture which quote the attributes of God (Exodus 34:6).

Psalm 146

Which God do you mean?

If someone asked you if you served God, you'd say "yes". But if they asked you: "Which god?", what would you say? We live in a world where the gods of the major religions are blurred into one, especially by the media, while it is quite clear that they're not the same. "God" is after all just a title. In verses 5-10 we have an excellent summary of who God is, or in other words, what name He goes by:

> I will speak of the glorious honour of thy majesty, and of thy wondrous works. And men shall speak of the might of thy terrible acts: and I will declare thy greatness. They shall abundantly utter the memory of thy great goodness, and shall sing of thy righteousness. **The LORD is gracious, and full of compassion; slow to anger, and of great mercy.** The LORD is good to all: and his tender mercies are over all his works. All thy works shall praise thee, O LORD; and thy saints shall bless thee. (Psalm 145:5-10)

Here's some more of the different parts of His name to think about:

- the God of Jacob
- the God who made heaven, the earth and the sea
- the God who executes judgement for the oppressed
- God who loves the righteous
- the God who relieves the fatherless and the widow
- God who upturns the way of the wicked

We can use these stated characteristics of God to explain who He is. Many who might call themselves Christians, for example, do not worship the God of Jacob (Jacob is the former name of Israel), choosing rather to ignore that aspect of Him. That's not the same god. Many choose to believe in evolution rather than the God who created the heaven, earth and sea. Not the same god. Many choose to create god in the image of a beneficent old gentleman who cares for the wicked and the good equally. Not the same god. Many have a god that they believe looks after their own financial affairs when in fact He cares more about the fatherless and the widow who may be afflicted because of their greed. Not the same god. So I think the question is not just about how we describe God to others, but about which god we ourselves worship.

Have we truly bothered to find out who He is?

Food for thought

Verse 7-8 - Like the previous Psalm, this Psalm describes or echoes the miraculous works of Jesus healing the woman with the issue of blood. For example, verse 7 "looseth" (Luke 13:12), verse 8 "bowed down" (Luke 13:11).

Verse 3 - Here the Psalmist voices a recurring theme in Scripture - that mankind cannot be relied upon - Psalm 118:8, Isaiah 31:3,

Jeremiah 17:5.

Psalm 147

A message for the invisible people

This Psalm is about the invisible people. It's about the outcasts; the ones who no-one notices. Do you feel like that sometimes? In verse 2, God gathers them:

> *The LORD doth build up Jerusalem: he gathereth together the outcasts of Israel. (Psalm 147:2)*

In verse 3, God heals them from their broken heart:

> *He healeth the broken in heart, and bindeth up their wounds. (Psalm 147:3)*

In verse 4, we see that He knows them all by name, no matter how small, or how hidden, or how insignificant they feel:

> *He telleth the number of the stars; he calleth them all by their names. (Psalm 147:4)*

In verse 6 He exalts the meek:

The LORD lifteth up the meek: he casteth the wicked down to the ground. (Psalm 147:6)

In verse 7 He makes grass to grow on the mountains where no-one can see it or access it — except for the lonely beasts that graze there:

Who covereth the heaven with clouds, who prepareth rain for the earth, who maketh grass to grow upon the mountains. (Psalm 147:8)

In verse 9 he feeds even the ravens no matter how far they are from civilisation:

He giveth to the beast his food, and to the young ravens which cry. (Psalm 147:9)

In verses 10-11 He tells us that He takes no pleasure in the measures of importance we use, but that His love is for those who serve Him, no matter how small they feel:

He delighteth not in the strength of the horse: he taketh not pleasure in the legs of a man. The LORD taketh pleasure in them that fear him, in those that hope in his mercy. (Psalm 147:10-11)

So if you feel small, alone, unworthy or forgotten, this Psalm is God's message to you.

Food for thought

Verse 9 - In saying that God feeds the ravens, we see the origin of Jesus' words in Matthew 6:26. But do we truly believe that God takes care of the birds? Or do we think that they live using their natural instincts? Scripture teaches that God cares for them and that this care He has for them should teach us that He will also care for us. If we think that the birds take care of themselves we will not truly appreciate the way that God cares for us.

Verse 11 - Do we consider that our actions may please God? Clearly it is the case that faithful behaviour does please Him just in the same way as when our children do as we wish we are pleased.

Psalm 148

Praising God

All the earth praises God. All His creation joins together in magnifying Him and exalting His greatness. In all of His creation we can see His magnificence, wisdom, and perfection. Everything works as it should, doing exactly what God intended it to do. The waves lap upon the beach, the tide goes out and comes in, the moon goes on its synchronous course, the dark descends and lifts again, animals wake, forage, eat, sleep. Day after day, hour after hour, here and there, everything declares God as perfect and praises His name.

Except us.

In verse 11 we see mankind taking their part in the daily continual praise of God. It is what should be happening, yet it never fully has been.

Since the mistake of Adam and Eve, mankind is the only part of God's creation to not fulfill the purpose for which He created it. We daily turn away from the path He has set for us. The sun, moon and stars, the seasons, the cycles of life all condemn us in our obstinacy.

Do any of them ever disobey or run off their course?

The song of praise of the whole earth is marred by us. That earth has been waiting for us to join it in praise:

> *For the earnest expectation of the creature waiteth for the manifestation of the sons of God. For the creature was made subject to vanity, not willingly, but by reason of him who hath subjected the same in hope, Because the creature itself also shall be delivered from the bondage of corruption into the glorious liberty of the children of God. For we know that the whole creation groaneth and travaileth in pain together until now. (Romans 8:19-22)*

We need a new song. The old song is torn and tattered, and ready for disposal. We have spoiled the perfect and harmonious creation of God. In Psalm 149 verse 1 the Psalmist praises God with a new song, a song sung in the assembly of saints:

> *Praise ye the LORD. Sing unto the LORD a new song, and his praise in the congregation of saints. (Psalm 149:1)*

It is the song sung by the new creation, a people born again and recreated, as we are if we are with Christ. It is those who are humble (v4) and have let go of their old life, embracing in meekness the life lived by grace. These new creatures sing a new song of praise, rejoining with the rest of creation, in one purpose and one common goal, that of Psalm 150 verse 6:

> *Let every thing that hath breath praise the LORD. Praise ye the LORD!*

Food for thought

Verse 4 - The "water that be above the heaven" quotes Genesis 1:7.

Verse 13 - Whilst we might think that the Psalm is speaking of God's excellent name in the context of the majesty of His creation, Hebrews 1:4 shows us that the one with the "excellent name" is the risen Jesus who we know to have a name above every name (see Philippians 2:9). So, even the majesty of creation is not as majestic as the work of salvation in Christ.

Psalm 149

The two-edged sword

For the word of God is quick, and powerful, and sharper than any **twoedged sword***, piercing even to the dividing asunder of soul and spirit, and of the joints and marrow, and is a discerner of the thoughts and intents of the heart. (Hebrews 4:12)*

Thus says the New Testament book of Hebrews, but why should we be considering it here? It is because the same phrase crops up in this Psalm:

Let the saints be joyful in glory: let them sing aloud upon their beds. Let the high praises of God be in their mouth, and **a twoedged sword in their hand***; To execute vengeance upon the heathen, and punishments upon the people; To bind their kings with chains, and their nobles with fetters of iron; To execute upon them the judgment written: this honour have all his saints. Praise ye the LORD. (Psalm 149:5-9)*

The word of God, when embodied in a person who understands and knows it, will pronounce righteous judgement. This is what Hebrews says. It is because the word is able to discern the hidden "thoughts and intents of the heart", because that's how God has designed it.

But it is most effective when used for our own heart, and our own intentions. This self examination is the subject of that chapter in Hebrews where we get the reference to the two-edged sword.

So, since the word of God is consistent, this must also be what the sword is in our Psalm — not a physical sword — but the ability of the word of God to discern the thoughts and intents of the heart.

It therefore stands to reason that what the Psalm is actually talking about is the saints of God being given the ability to look into the hearts of others and to discern the thoughts and intentions they see there. If this prophecy is speaking of the Kingdom age, it means that there will be no place to hide for those who continue to hate the Lord Jesus, and despise the righteous laws he instigates.

But there is a reason to believe that the Psalm *isn't* talking about the Kingdom age, but just before. Look at this passage again and see if you notice anything odd:

> *Let the saints be joyful in glory: let them sing aloud upon their beds. Let the high praises of God be in their mouth, and a twoedged sword in their hand; (Psalm 149:5-6)*

Did you spot the reference to the saints in their beds? Well, in the Kingdom age, saints will have no need for beds, for:

> *For when they shall rise from the dead, they neither marry, nor are given in marriage; but are **as the angels** which are in heaven. (Mark 12:25)*

So this Psalm may be speaking of a time before the Kingdom, when the Saints, for whatever reason, are given the responsibility for triggering God's judgements on the world that have been so long prophesied.

Whether or not that is the case, it seems from other prophecies that this judgement role will certainly be there in the Kingdom age:

> *Do ye not know that the saints shall judge the world? and if the world shall be judged by you, are ye unworthy to judge the smallest matters? (1 Corinthians 6:2)*

Food for thought

Verse 1 - The "children of Zion" are not literally those who live in Zion. Rather it is to do with birth and allegiance – Psalm 87:3-6.

Verse 2 - The "children of Zion" should include us if we are part of the multitude who are "free" Gal 4:26.

Psalm 150

Praise God in His sanctuary

Where is the "sanctuary" mentioned in verse 1, where we ought to praise God?

> *Praise ye the LORD. Praise God in his **sanctuary**: praise him in the firmament of his power. (Psalm 150:1)*

The Hebrew word "sanctuary" is usually translated "Holy", such as in its first occurrence in the Bible:

> *And the angel of the LORD appeared unto him in a flame of fire out of the midst of a bush: and he looked, and, behold, the bush burned with fire, and the bush was not consumed. ... And he said, Draw not nigh hither: put off thy shoes from off thy feet, for the place whereon thou standest is **holy** ground. (Exodus 3:2, 5)*

So it's not necessarily speaking of a separate place, but a nearness to God. In the case of Moses and the burning bush, it was the ground around the presence of the angel that was holy, and where Moses had to alter his behaviour to signify his humility and obedience.

With our prayers and praise, is it possible that there is a state of mind, of reverence and tranquillity, that we could say is set apart for God? It would be a state of mind that recognises that God's name, purpose and character are Holy and separate.

If God is separate and Holy, we need to get to know who God is through His word rather than assuming who He is. Thus while this Psalm seems to be advocating praise without any limits, it is in fact referring to specific instruments and songs. These were ordained by the prophet David to be played and sung in front of the Ark of the LORD:

> *And he appointed certain of the Levites to minister before the ark of the LORD, and to record, and to thank and praise the LORD God of Israel... with psalteries and with harps; but Asaph made a sound with cymbals; Benaiah also and Jahaziel the priests with trumpets continually before the ark of the covenant of God. Then on that day David delivered first this Psalm to thank the LORD into the hand of Asaph and his brethren. Give thanks unto the LORD, call upon his name, make known his deeds among the people. Sing unto him, sing Psalms unto him, talk ye of all his wondrous works. (1 Chronicles 16:4-9)*

These were specifically appointed people, specifically appointed instruments, and specifically commissioned songs. Once the Ark was placed in its tent, David set up ministers to "do according to all that is written in the law of the LORD, which he commanded Israel". In other words, to be fully obedient to the word of God:

> *So he left there before the ark of the covenant of the LORD Asaph*

*and his brethren, to minister before the ark continually, as every day's work required ... To offer burnt offerings unto the LORD upon the altar of the burnt offering continually morning and evening, and **to do according to all that is written in the law of the LORD, which he commanded Israel.** (1 Chronicles 16:37, 40)*

For us there are no set songs or set prayers, since we are able to approach God in prayer through our high priest, the Lord Jesus. Yet the Psalm draws on what David did, and if we are to praise God as the Psalm requires, we are to do so with minds set apart to God. These minds must be prepared by reading, meditating on, and understanding God's word. This is how we can praise God in His sanctuary.

Let every thing that hath breath praise the LORD.

Praise ye the LORD.

Food for thought

Note - The Psalms 146, 147, 148, 149, 150 all end with "praise ye the Lord", in Hebrew 'Hallelujah.' This is the end of all things. Whatever else we think we must realise that we have got to praise the Lord for all that he has done for us. Not merely saying the word 'Hallelujah' but transforming our lives into a "sacrifice of praise" (see Hebrews 13:15), which is the song of the redeemed (Revelation 19:1, 3, 4, 6).

Verse 6 - Having worked through the musical instruments that might be used to praise God, the ultimate is given. Everything should praise Him. We can take the encouragement to ourselves that God desires *our* praise and thanks, no matter how good our singing voice may be!

Epilogue

The Psalms have taken us all the way from the glories of creation, through the building of God's Kingdom of Israel, to the thoughts of the Lord Jesus on the cross. They have given us comfort in our own trials and struggles, and pointed us to salvation by faith in Jesus.

Finally, we have ended with the glories of the coming Kingdom on earth, where (by grace) we will be able to praise God forevermore.

> *Praise ye the LORD. Praise God in his sanctuary: praise him in the firmament of his power. Praise him for his mighty acts: praise him according to his excellent greatness. Praise him with the sound of the trumpet: praise him with the psaltery and harp. Praise him with the timbrel and dance: praise him with stringed instruments and organs. Praise him upon the loud cymbals: praise him upon the high sounding cymbals. Let every thing that hath breath praise the LORD. Praise ye the LORD. (Psalm 150:1-6)*

Let's resolve to live a life of praise in preparation for this wonderful time.

Other books in the series

If you have enjoyed *Food for thought in the Psalms* then why not sign up for news about other books in the series?

The *Food for thought in the Old Testament* series aims to build up into a library of books covering each chapter in the Old Testament of the Bible.

Sign up here for publication announcements and exclusive offers:
   www.woodland.press/sign-up

OTHER BOOKS IN THE SERIES

- Genesis
- Joshua
- Ezra, Nehemiah & Esther
- Jeremiah & Lamentations
- Exodus
- Judges & Ruth
- Job
- Ezekiel
- Leviticus
- 1 & 2 Samuel
- Psalms ✓
- Daniel & Hosea
- Numbers
- 1 & 2 Kings
- Proverbs, Ecclesiastes & Song of Solomon
- Joel to Nahum
- Deuteronomy
- 1 & 2 Chronicles
- Isaiah
- Habakkuk to Malachi

Index

A

Aaron 38, 70, 163, 194, 257-58, 298-99, 340, 342
  Abel 324, 334
  Abiathar 86, 305
  Abiram 116-17
  Abishai 328
  Abraham 67, 195, 205, 223, 239-40, 264, 272-73, 276, 299, 334
  Absalom 10, 16, 21, 115, 142, 165-67, 180, 228, 284
  Adam 77, 130, 322, 334, 377
  Adonijah 86
  Adullam 147, 360
  adultery 16, 78, 96, 141, 269
  afflict 55, 72, 82, 171, 197-98, 215, 227, 311, 332, 356-57, 363, 372
  Ahaz 316
  Ahaziah 126
  Ahimelech 263
  Ahithophel 10, 142, 168, 284, 323
  Altaschith 147, 150, 152
  angel 6, 83, 114-15, 159, 176-77, 236-37, 253, 271, 275, 324, 381, 383
  apple 41, 237
  Asahel 85-86, 328

Asaph 191-92, 195, 201-2, 207, 214, 384
Asarelah 201
Assyria 55-56, 255, 260
avenge 20, 245-46

B

Baalhamon 210
  Babylon 126, 202, 275, 314, 326, 349
  Baca 218
  backsliding 138
  Bakbukiah 202
  Balaam 281
  Bathsheba 14, 17, 78, 133, 156, 185, 269, 362
  Bedouin 315
  beds 343, 380-81
  Benaiah 384
  Bethlehem 339
  betrayal 44, 106, 139-40, 142, 284
  boar 209
  Boaz 41, 236
  boil 96-97
  bow 27, 29, 74, 167, 198, 253
  branch 209, 240
  bread 33, 105-6, 131, 137, 165, 287, 357
  bride 315, 357
  brokenhearted 283
  building 61, 164, 329, 331, 386
  bunker 65
  butter 141, 166

C

Cain 334
  Caleb 56, 234, 237
  calf 268
  camels 314-15
  Canaan 138, 176, 199, 210, 272, 289, 297, 314, 322
  cave 84, 147-48, 312, 328, 358, 360, 365
  cedar 70, 209, 225, 339
  centurion 205
  Chaldean 208, 349
  chasten 16, 96, 100-101, 159, 186, 192, 195, 246, 248, 284, 362
  Cherethites 20
  cherubim 258, 334
  Chronicles 26, 114-15, 126, 207, 230, 274-75, 287, 326-27, 337, 349-50, 384-85
  cloud 69, 257-58, 375
  Colossians 134, 267
  comfort 21, 32, 54-56, 173, 179-82, 284, 292, 343, 386
  commandment 97, 289-90, 309-10, 366
  conception 92
  congregation 38, 62, 92, 102, 117, 163, 171, 194-95, 214-15, 243, 342, 378
  Corinthians 22, 93, 291-92, 341, 348, 382
  covenant 59, 94, 116, 131, 164, 192, 223, 225, 272, 290, 324-25, 334, 338, 384
  creation 21, 70, 81, 248, 343, 377-79, 386
  creator 22, 214, 295, 323
  crucify 7, 54, 180
  cymbals 201, 384, 386
  Cyrus 327

D

dance 73, 145

Daniel 81, 173, 198, 275, 350

Dathan 116-17

David 5-6, 8-12, 14-17, 19-21, 24, 28-32, 36-41, 43-44, 47-49, 51-53, 55-56, 58-62, 64-68, 72-76, 78, 82, 84-87, 89-92, 96-98, 100-101, 104-6, 111-15, 118, 120, 125, 129-30, 133-35, 137-42, 144-50, 152-53, 155-58, 160-68, 171-72, 179-83, 185, 187-88, 192, 200-201, 206, 219, 223-26, 228, 230, 237, 245-46, 262-64, 269, 281-84, 287, 298, 300-301, 303-5, 307-11, 313, 315, 317-18, 322-23, 328-29, 331, 335-41, 353-56, 358-66, 368, 384-85

deaf 150-51

deceit 57-58, 91, 131, 142, 150, 153, 262-63, 314, 355

devour 34, 209, 211

dew 67, 340

disciples 8-9, 17, 44, 169-70, 172, 240, 307, 319

distress 8, 11, 40, 43-44, 75, 87, 124, 139, 142, 160, 166, 179-80, 300, 314, 365

Dodavah 126

Doeg 120, 135-36, 263, 304-5

dwell 8-9, 35-36, 52, 56, 61, 64-65, 75, 106, 136, 160, 169, 219, 225, 240, 258, 262, 294, 314, 321, 339, 354

dwelling 64-65, 98, 129, 135-36, 144, 160, 176, 208, 224-25, 237-38, 315, 321, 338

E

eagle's 268

Ecclesiastes 36, 101, 200, 359

Eden 334

Edom 120, 135-36, 155, 199, 263, 266-67, 281-82, 305, 349-50
Egypt 49, 56, 69, 97, 176, 194, 199-200, 202, 204-6, 209-10, 212-13, 223, 225, 234, 238, 243, 259, 275, 295-97, 345-46, 348
Eliezer 126
Elim 113
encamp 33, 83, 113
En-Gedi 365
Enoch 168
Ephesians 13, 22
ephod 305
Ephratah 339
eternal 57-58, 117, 240, 311
Ethan 259
Eve 77, 130, 377
evil 24-26, 30, 36, 47, 52, 55-56, 62, 87, 91, 93, 103-4, 117, 131, 138, 146, 168, 213, 246, 252-53, 274, 283, 292, 325, 334, 357
evolution 372
Exodus 35, 39, 44, 49, 58, 60, 112-13, 162-64, 177, 196, 199, 210, 213, 223, 230, 253, 258, 269, 273, 292, 295-97, 313, 340, 345-46, 366-67, 370, 383
Ezekiel 4, 243, 249, 315, 331
Eziongeber 126
Ezra 48, 269, 329
Ezrahite 259

F

faith 9-10, 14, 32, 49-50, 57-58, 65-66, 81, 83-84, 102, 117-18, 121, 126, 136, 159, 185, 193, 205-6, 223, 225, 228, 234, 237, 239, 243, 272-73, 276, 292, 311, 313, 325, 331, 333, 348, 359, 361, 363, 376, 386

families 11, 117, 201, 369
fasting 284
fatherless 26, 176, 214-15, 245, 372
fellowship 30, 68, 344, 348
firstborn 159, 177, 324, 345
flatter 14, 29, 34, 91, 93
flood 23, 43, 70-71, 78, 227, 233-34, 242, 271
footstool 338
forever 129, 136, 160, 239, 310-11, 347, 386
fortress 74-75, 365
foundation 49, 213, 229, 265-66, 270, 349
fruitful 92, 210-11, 331

G

gabahh 336
Gad 75
Galal 202
Galatians 226, 325
Galilee 8
gall 180
garment 265-66, 287, 340
gate 39, 86, 180, 224, 318, 328
Gath 20, 84, 144-46
Gedaliah 201
Genesis 23, 67, 69-71, 78, 81, 137-38, 168, 178, 206, 223, 233, 240, 261, 264, 271, 273, 276, 281, 299, 335, 339, 379
Gentile 94, 205, 243, 250, 259-60, 302, 343, 345
Gethsemane 104, 113, 181, 283
giant 138, 144-45
Gibeah 6

Gibeon 114
Gideon 217
Gilboa 67
Gittite 20-21
gnash 86, 205, 292
Goliath 144, 339
Gomorrah 136
goodness 83, 103, 169, 247, 260, 279, 327, 363, 368-69, 371
gospel 81, 117, 121, 175, 259-60, 311, 325, 368
grace 47, 98, 120, 156, 269, 279, 291-92, 325, 363, 371, 378, 386
Greeks 348
grow 3-4, 16, 21, 214, 233, 267
guilt 62, 269, 286-87

H

Habakkuk 28, 244
  habitation 61, 64-65, 80, 176, 199, 274, 321, 339
  Hallelujah 385
  Hannah 294
  Hanun 156
  Hashabiah 201
  heaven 27, 65, 69, 80, 98, 131, 137, 148, 159-60, 177, 182, 195, 200, 205, 209, 213, 222-23, 229, 238-39, 242-43, 265-67, 294, 309-11, 323-25, 327, 348, 350, 354, 361, 372, 375, 379, 381
  Hebrew 24, 46, 214, 304, 320, 334-36, 346, 366, 383, 385
  Hebrews 6-7, 81, 119, 159, 238, 244, 248, 253, 271-72, 305, 324-25, 337, 379-81, 385
  Hebron 6, 86
  heifer 134, 285-86
  Hermon 111, 340-41

INDEX

Hezekiah 96-98, 207, 254-55, 260, 274-75, 316, 320-21, 333
Hiram 125
Hittite 155
holy 5, 27-28, 35, 61, 114-15, 117, 126, 163, 169, 176, 192, 194, 199, 207, 238, 248, 254, 260, 272, 274, 282, 289-90, 340-41, 364, 383-84
honey 48, 166, 234
honeycomb 357
Horeb 366
humble 19, 24, 88-90, 100, 182-83, 186, 248, 294-95, 336-37, 352, 378, 384
hunger 82, 166, 268, 309, 357
Hushai 168
hyssop 134

I

idolatry 212-13, 252-53, 275, 298-99, 317
Idumea 267, 350
iniquity 17-18, 33, 47, 91-92, 96, 99-100, 103, 137, 152, 163, 167, 172, 219-20, 223, 241, 246, 257, 269, 274-75, 306, 313, 334, 359, 366
inquisition 23-24
instruments 145, 328, 384-86
inward 14, 167, 250
Isaac 205, 240, 272-73
Isaiah 47, 55-56, 90, 94, 97, 101, 122, 173, 188, 197-98, 210, 213, 230, 243, 266-67, 305, 316, 321, 350, 372
Israel 5, 10, 19, 30, 33-34, 38, 41, 44, 49, 65, 69, 87, 95, 112-13, 115-16, 118, 131-32, 135, 138, 145, 151, 171, 174-77, 192, 194, 199-200, 202, 204-6, 208, 210, 212-13, 215-17, 225, 234, 236, 238, 243, 247, 249-50, 254, 257-58, 260, 266-67, 272, 274-76, 281-82,

286-87, 289, 296-99, 314, 318, 322, 325, 327, 331-33, 338, 340, 343, 345-46, 348, 358, 366, 372, 374, 384-86
  Ittai 21
  ivory 125

J

Jacob 33-34, 49, 122, 124, 171, 205, 220, 224, 255, 272, 281-82, 296, 338-39, 372
  Jael 178
  Jahaziel 384
  James 101, 168, 186, 359
  Japheth 315
  Javan 315
  Jebus 114-15
  Jeduthun 201-2
  Jehoshaphat 126, 336
  Jeremiah 55, 58, 126, 136, 151, 195, 207, 314-15, 327, 333, 355, 373
  Jericho 322
  Jerusalem 6, 21, 106, 115, 122, 125-27, 159, 176-77, 197, 200, 207-8, 224-26, 254-55, 260, 265-66, 288, 302, 318-19, 324, 327, 333, 349-50, 374
  Jeshaiah 201
  Jesse 187
  Jesus 6-8, 17-18, 34, 36, 43-44, 53-54, 57-58, 73-76, 87, 89, 94, 98-99, 101-4, 113, 117, 119-22, 127, 130-32, 134, 142, 159, 161, 169, 172, 179-83, 188, 194, 205, 210, 213, 215, 219, 221-22, 225, 230, 236-37, 239-40, 244, 246-47, 249-51, 253, 255, 260, 283-84, 286-88, 301-2, 305, 307, 309, 311, 315, 324, 335, 348, 363, 372, 376, 379, 381, 385-86

Joab 85-86, 135, 155-56, 328
John 39, 87, 104, 172, 215, 219, 251, 253, 307, 311
Jonah 25, 180, 227, 355
Jonah's 180, 227
Jonathan 105-6
Jordan 111, 296, 322-23, 341
Joseph 201
Joshua 35-36, 56, 90, 140, 234, 237, 296-97, 314, 322-23
joyful 124, 126, 230, 247-48, 259, 294-95, 380-81
Judah 75, 126, 140, 164-65, 200, 207, 255, 260, 266, 275, 318, 327, 337
Judas 284
Jude 228
judges 25, 49, 162, 178, 217, 279, 296, 332-33
juniper 314
justice 140-41, 175, 215, 230, 286-87, 356
justify 194, 206, 362-63

K

Kedar 314-15
Kidron 165
kindled 6
kindness 60, 105, 302-3
kingdom 6, 36, 58, 119, 157, 175, 182, 205, 237, 248, 260, 282, 288, 309, 318-19, 325, 327, 331, 361, 381-82, 386
kings 5-6, 26, 80, 151, 174, 187, 200, 253, 275, 287, 303, 343, 350, 380
Kiss 5-6, 221-22
knee 52, 77, 97, 253, 312
Kohathites 192

Korah 91-92, 111, 116-17, 122, 220, 228

L

lamb 183
  Lamech 168, 233
  Lamentations 126, 132
  Lehi 332
  Levi 38-39, 285
  Levite 37-38, 384
  Leviticus 10, 211, 341-42
  liberty 292, 308-9, 378
  lion 82, 148-49, 172, 237, 273, 328
  lovingkindness 41, 62, 102, 133, 166, 365
  lowly 183, 351
  Luke 7, 17, 34, 75, 120, 130, 142, 222, 236-37, 255, 268, 372

M

Mahol 259
  maiden 320-21, 349
  Mary 255, 301
  Maschil 111, 139, 142, 195, 263, 358
  Mattaniah 202
  Matthew 4, 7, 17, 34, 44, 54, 58, 68, 75-76, 89, 113, 132, 161, 169, 180-81, 241, 249, 280, 309, 315, 319, 333, 361, 376
  Mattithiah 202
  mediate 98, 324
  meditate 3, 9, 39, 52, 62, 74, 128, 164, 239, 311, 385
  Melchisedek 39, 287
  Mephibosheth 105-6

mercy 11, 19, 31, 51, 60, 78, 98, 133, 142, 144, 147-48, 153, 160, 162, 164, 172, 174, 183, 199, 202, 221-23, 228, 230, 254-55, 261, 265, 269, 286-87, 299, 302-3, 320, 347, 363, 368, 371, 375
- **Meshech** 314-15
- **Mesopotamia** 156
- **Messiah** 188, 221
- **Methuselah** 233
- **Micah** 182-83, 207, 252, 255, 333, 339
- **Micha** 202
- **Michal** 153
- **Michtam** 144, 147, 152, 156
- **Midianite** 276
- **Mizar** 111
- **Moab** 55, 75, 199, 281-82
- **Morasthite** 207
- **Moses** 35, 39, 44, 52, 70, 90-92, 107, 112, 114, 116-17, 183, 194, 196, 199-200, 223, 226, 234, 237, 257-58, 275, 287, 292, 313, 325, 346, 366, 383
  - **mountains** 67, 121, 176, 252, 255, 271, 340, 375
  - **mourn** 73, 112, 182, 227, 333
  - **murder** 23-24, 96, 141, 148, 245, 286-87, 304
  - **musician** 89, 111, 122, 133, 139, 144, 147, 152, 156, 174, 201, 220, 263, 353

N

Nabal 26
- **Nathan** 133, 339
- **Nebuchadrezzar** 314
- **Neginoth** 139, 174
- **Nehemiah** 132, 201-2, 343

neighbour 29, 36, 136, 193, 263
Nethaniah 201
Noah 23, 70-71, 78, 137-38

O

oath 272, 275
  Obadiah 350
  ointment 340
  oppress 25, 112, 139, 144, 215, 372

P

palace 16, 21, 208, 350
  Palestine 199, 315
  parable 75, 102-4, 128, 130, 161, 210-11, 222, 268
  pavilion 64-65
  peace 8-9, 148, 221, 230, 248, 314, 321, 331, 333, 361
  Pelethites 20
  Persia 327
  Pharaoh 58, 199, 345-46
  Pharisees 211, 302
  Philippians 36, 295, 379
  Philistine 20, 144-46, 332
  Phinehas 276
  plague 58, 136, 191-92, 204, 237, 273, 276, 345-46
  planted 3-4, 209-11, 239-40
  praise 21, 32, 51-52, 61, 67, 72-73, 81, 103, 115, 123-24, 171-72, 199, 202, 238, 243-44, 247, 259-60, 265, 274, 279, 282, 289, 294, 302, 309, 347, 354, 366, 368-69, 371, 377-78, 380-81, 383-86
  pray 11, 15, 18-19, 32, 40-41, 44, 51-52, 68, 77-78, 83, 88, 104,

112-15, 117, 121, 133, 152-54, 164, 172, 179-80, 187-88, 194-95, 202, 205, 223, 227-28, 245, 274-75, 281, 283-84, 294, 301, 309, 333, 343, 350, 353, 355-56, 358, 362, 364, 369, 384-85
preach 260, 368
priest 37, 61, 86, 98, 135-36, 208, 211, 238, 245, 257, 285, 287, 304-5, 340, 342, 384-85
prison 130
prophecy 6, 43, 53-54, 74, 76, 87, 119, 126, 135-36, 169, 179, 187-88, 201-2, 207, 221, 252, 265, 281-83, 286, 321, 327, 350, 381-82
prophet 66, 75, 97, 119, 133, 208, 273, 333, 339, 384
proverbs 29, 48, 128, 138, 186, 246, 289-90, 348, 356-57
provocation 247
psaltery 201, 384, 386
punish 47, 116, 135, 156, 380

Q

queen 174-75, 187-88

R

Rabbah 156
  Rahab 242-43, 297
  ravens 375-76
  reaping 102
  rebel 115-16, 151, 228, 275
  rebuke 9, 16, 96, 100-101, 209, 225, 230, 271, 359
  redeem 24, 44, 75, 129-30, 199, 202, 269, 286-87, 290, 341, 363, 385
  refuge 25, 33, 64-65, 78, 121-22, 147, 153, 164, 218, 360, 365
  reins 39, 354

rejoice 31, 33-34, 51, 67, 75, 103, 164-65, 170, 355

remember 10, 16, 19, 24, 96, 142, 144, 205, 216, 254-55, 272, 326, 346

remission, of sins 363

reproach 36, 53, 148, 179, 283-84

rib 85-86

righteous 4, 9, 11, 18-19, 27, 30, 33-35, 57-58, 82-83, 94-95, 102, 119, 131, 141-42, 162, 168, 185, 187-88, 206, 221, 227, 248, 255, 263, 273, 276, 291, 309, 313, 325, 331-32, 359, 361-63, 368, 371-72, 380-81

rivers 4, 239, 326

Romans 48, 73, 78, 95, 177, 206, 341, 352, 357, 363, 378

S

Sabbath 241, 308-9

sackcloth 321

sacrifice 9, 114, 131, 134, 140, 192, 287, 301, 341, 385

saints 82, 131, 221, 229, 242-43, 253, 371, 378, 380-82

salvation 10, 31, 33-34, 51, 57, 65, 85, 95, 102-3, 130, 161, 166, 170, 204, 220, 223, 244, 252, 254, 259, 271, 334, 341, 345, 348, 368, 379, 386

Samaria 6

Samson 39, 332

Samuel 5, 12, 26, 35-36, 39, 43, 52, 75, 84, 120, 135, 139, 142, 144, 153, 155-56, 166, 168, 179-80, 200, 206, 225, 230, 257-58, 263, 287, 300, 305, 323, 329, 336, 339, 361-62, 366

sanctuary 163-64, 166, 191-92, 343, 349, 383, 385-86

Sarah 240

Saul 28, 31, 67-68, 73-75, 105, 139, 144-45, 147-50, 152-53, 165, 245-46, 263, 300, 304-5, 328, 336, 360-61

sceptre 119, 281-82

scorn 3, 53-54, 62, 320-21

Seba 187

secret 64-65, 106, 168, 354

Selah 8, 13, 78, 100, 122, 124, 130-31, 135, 139, 148, 160, 174, 177, 220, 224, 362

Sennacherib 254-55, 320-21

serpent 130, 150

servant 12, 20-21, 35, 38, 46, 58, 65, 89-90, 102, 142, 144-45, 148, 152-53, 155, 157, 184, 205, 211, 222, 225, 230, 238, 241, 272, 275, 280, 295, 301, 305, 320-21, 325, 333, 336, 342-43, 345, 362-63, 366

shadow 41, 55-56, 147, 158, 164, 209, 237-39, 316

shake 53, 72, 325

Shammua 202

Sheba (see also Seba) 174-75, 187-88

sheep 65, 86, 129, 149, 166, 183, 195, 245, 249, 260

Sheminith 16

shepherd 183, 339

shield 21, 67-68, 236, 365

shining 175, 313, 354

ships 125-26

Shur 112

shut 179, 342

sick 97

siege 266

Silas 309

sin 3, 8, 13-14, 16-17, 26, 44, 46-47, 58-59, 62, 73, 77-78, 96-100, 104, 117, 120, 133-34, 141-42, 152, 156-57, 168, 202, 213, 220, 222-23, 234, 241, 269, 274-75, 306-7, 334-35, 341, 343, 362-63

Sinai 176-77, 202, 325

singing 31, 123-24, 145, 188, 326, 385

Sion (see also Zion) 159, 177, 324
slander 29, 131, 263
slaughter 145, 183
slave 204, 341
Sleep 8
slothful 102
slumber 317, 338
smite 56, 97, 135, 281, 314, 366
snares 28, 43, 168, 359-60
Sodom 136, 138
Solomon 6, 66, 125-26, 128, 174-75, 185, 187-88, 192, 200, 210, 225, 230, 259, 290, 303, 315, 318, 331, 342, 350, 357, 359
sorrow 31, 37, 43-44, 78, 199, 234, 301
sparrows 103
spear 68, 85, 148, 328
spies 138, 237
staff 55-56
stars 374, 377
Stephen 213, 292, 302
steps 11, 24, 68, 116, 146, 148, 313
stork 195
storm 169
stranger 139, 245, 250, 284
stronghold 224
sword 21, 54, 115, 141, 148, 167, 172, 245, 267, 328, 349-50, 380-81
Syria 156
Syriamaachah 156

T

tabernacle 35, 38, 64-65, 114-16, 160, 163, 191-92, 211, 225, 238, 258, 288, 338, 342
  tables 313
  talent 102-3, 156, 188
  Tarshish 125-26, 187
  teeth 86, 148, 205, 292, 328
  tempest 9, 28, 176
  temple 4, 27-28, 61, 64-66, 114, 169, 191-92, 207, 225, 318, 339, 342-43
  testimony 156, 163, 244, 257, 306, 310, 342
  thorns 304
  threshingfloor 114
  timbrel 386
  tithes 38
  tongue 14, 36, 53, 101, 131, 148, 167-68, 172, 262, 314, 326, 328, 353, 357, 359
  tower 65, 145, 158, 160, 210, 365
  transgress 40, 46, 133, 141, 152, 157, 208, 223, 275
  trumpet 384, 386
  trust 6, 9, 25-26, 31-32, 41-42, 49-51, 59, 65, 67-68, 77-78, 83, 94, 103, 105, 118, 129-30, 142, 146-47, 160, 164, 192, 204, 206, 221, 236, 262, 298, 301, 310, 324, 327, 331, 355-56, 358-59
  truth 14, 35, 59, 62, 75, 102, 114-15, 148, 160, 170, 196, 221, 230, 236, 244, 254, 261-62, 290, 302, 317, 366
  Tubal 315
  tumult 169, 321
  turtledove 195
  Tyrus 243

U

ungodly 3, 15, 43, 62, 115, 206
  upright 27, 29, 35, 46, 129, 157, 219, 290
  Uriah 133, 155-56

V

vanity 29, 57, 100, 367, 378
  vengeance 24, 245, 257, 350, 380
  vessels 192, 208, 315, 349-50
  vine 209-11, 240, 267, 331
  vinegar 180
  vow 36, 160, 171-72, 200, 338

W

waves 9, 111, 169, 227-30, 242-43, 377
  wax 53, 252, 265-66
  wealth 42, 125, 129-30, 321
  weary 166, 177, 219
  weep 19, 44, 165, 205, 218-19, 284, 326
  wicked 14, 25-27, 29-30, 47, 62, 78, 91, 93, 102, 117, 119-20, 138, 150, 156, 161, 167-68, 191, 193, 195, 197, 246, 253, 274-75, 292, 311, 325, 332, 353, 357, 359, 366, 372, 375
  widow 34, 176, 236, 245, 372
  wilderness 19, 112, 114, 142, 164-66, 169, 177, 194, 204, 206, 234-35, 237-38, 247, 258, 260, 290, 366
  winepress 210
  wings 41, 147, 160, 164, 236-37, 354
  wise 14, 75, 88-91, 101, 126, 128, 146, 150, 161, 174, 223, 244, 259, 262, 289-90, 331, 348, 377
  wives 11, 21, 116, 165

worship 73, 114, 140, 162-64, 212, 252-53, 258, 302-3, 309, 317, 319, 338, 372
wound 11, 96, 168, 178, 243, 285, 374
wrath 6, 96, 142, 208, 220, 287

Y

yoke 183

Z

Zabdi 202
  Zaccur 201
  Zalmunna 217
  Zaretan 322
  zeal 284
  Zeba 217
  Zechariah 188, 221, 266, 288
  Zephaniah 66
  Zeruiah 328
  Ziba 106, 165
  Zion (see also Sion) 5, 33-34, 52, 56, 73, 115, 125-26, 132, 176, 207, 224-26, 251, 255, 258, 260, 265-66, 287, 324-26, 331, 339-41, 344, 350, 382
  Ziph 139-40
  Zoan 205
  Zobah 156

About the Author

Rob de Jongh is a lifelong Bible student and has been sharing his perspective on the Bible through talks, studies and group work for the last 20 years. He has written over one thousand Bible studies and has become known for his fresh perspective, accessible writing style, and ability to make the Bible relevant. He formerly worked as a non-fiction editor alongside some of the world's best educators, and helped to devise bestselling books for two successive publishers. Catch up with him at www.woodland.press

www.ingramcontent.com/pod-product-compliance
Lightning Source LLC
Chambersburg PA
CBHW071553080526
44588CB00010B/896